How to Stop Overthinking

---

27 Proven Ways to Rewire Your Anxious Brain, Calm Your Thoughts, Stop Worrying, and Be Happy

Layla Moon

How to Stop Overthinking

PUBLISHED BY: Layla Moon

©Copyright 2021 - All rights reserved.

All rights reserved. No part of this publication may be reproduced, distributed, or transmitted in any form or by any means, including photocopying, recording, or other electronic or mechanical methods, without the prior written permission of the publisher, except in the case of brief quotations embodied in critical reviews and certain other noncommercial uses permitted by copyright law.

Under no circumstances will any blame or legal responsibility be held against the publisher, or author, for any damages, reparation, or monetary loss due to the information contained within this book, either directly or indirectly.

Legal Notice:

This book is copyright protected. It is only for personal use. You cannot amend, distribute, sell, use, quote or paraphrase any part, or the content within this book, without the consent of the author or publisher.

Disclaimer Notice:

Please note the information contained within this document is for educational and entertainment purposes only. All effort has been executed to present accurate, up to date, reliable, complete information. No warranties of any kind are declared or implied. Readers acknowledge that the author is not engaged in the rendering of legal, financial, medical or professional advice. The content within this book has been derived from various sources. Please consult a licensed professional before attempting any techniques outlined in this book.

By reading this document, the reader agrees that under no circumstances is the author responsible for any losses, direct or indirect, that are incurred as a result of the use of the information contained within this document, including, but not limited to, errors, omissions, or inaccuracies.

How to Stop Overthinking

Table of Contents

4 FREE Gifts	1
Introduction	7
Chapter One: Finding Your Foundations	15
Chapter Two: Methods for Managing Stress	27
Method 1: The 5-4-3-2-1 Grounding Technique	29
Method 2: Deep Breathing Away the Stress	33
Method 3: Understand the Causes of Your Stress	38
Method 4: Keeping a Stress Journal	44
Method 5: Mastering Autogenic Training	49
Method 6: How to Get Focused and Avoid Procrastination	53
Method 7: How to Deal with Stressful External Factors	60
Chapter Three: Methods for Managing Anxiety	65
Method 8: Muscle Relaxation Techniques	67
Method 9: How to Deal with Negative Thinking in the Moment	70

Method 10: How to Stop a Panic Attack — 76

Method 11: Reaching Out to Friends, Family, and Getting Support — 80

Method 12: Lifestyle Tips to Help You Overcome Anxiety — 85

Chapter Four: Methods for Calming an Overthinking Mind — 90

Method 13: Developing the Habit of Meditation — 91

Method 14: Being Able to Consciously Think — 95

Method 15: How to Use CBT Training — 100

Method 16: How to Deal with Fears and Worries — 106

Method 17: Seeking Therapy and Professional Services — 111

Chapter Five: Methods for Happiness and Rewiring Your Mind — 116

Method 18: The Art of Helping Others That Ends Up Helping You — 117

Method 19: Becoming a Social Butterfly — 122

Method 20: Developing Your Positive Self Talk — 127

Method 21: Setting Goals and Having Aspirations — 130

Method 22: Only Focusing on What You Have Control Over… — 137

Method 23: …& Finding Peace With Everything Else — 144

Method 24: Discovering the Joys of Gratitude — 149

Method 25: The Simple Act of Setting Up Your Day — 157

Method 26: Working on Habits That Will Take Care of You — 162

Method 27: Truly Live in the Moment — 168

Final Thoughts — 171

Thank you — 173

References — 174

4 FREE Gifts

To help you along your spiritual journey, I've created 4 FREE bonus eBooks.

You can get instant access by signing up to my email newsletter below.

On top of the 4 free books, you will also receive weekly tips along with free book giveaways, discounts, and so much more.

All of these bonuses are 100% free with no strings attached. You don't need to provide any personal information except your email address.

To get your bonus, go to:

https://dreamlifepress.com/four-free-gifts

Or scan the QR code below

Spirit Guides for Beginners: How to Hear the Universe's Call and Communicate with Your Spirit Guide and Guardian Angels

Guided by Moon herself, inspired by her own experiences and knowledge that has been passed down by hundreds of generations for thousands of years, you'll discover everything you need to know to;

- Understanding what the call of the universe is
- How to hear and comprehend it
- Knowing who and what your spirit guides and guardian angels are
- Learning how to connect, start a conversation, and listen to your guides
- How to manifest your dreams with the help of the cosmic source
- Learning how to start living the life you want to live
- And so much more…

Law of Attraction: Manifest Your Desire

Learn how to tap into the infinite power of the universe and manifest everything you want in life.

Includes:

- Law of Attraction: Manifest Your Desire ebook
- Law of Attraction Workbook
- Cheat sheets and checklists so make sure you're on the right path

Hoodoo Book of Spells for Beginners: Easy and effective Rootwork, Conjuring, and Protection Spells for Healing and Prosperity

Harness the power of one of the greatest magics. Hoodoo is a powerful force ideal for holding negativity at bay, promoting positivity in all areas in your life, offering protection to the things you love, and ultimately taking control of your destiny.

Inside, you will discover:
- How to get started with Hoodoo in your day-to-day life
- How to use conjuration spells to manifest the life you want to live
- How casting protection spells can help you withstand the toughest of times
- Break cycles of bad luck and promote good fortune throughout your life
- Hoodoo to encourage prosperity and financial stability
- How to heal using Hoodoo magic, both short-term and long-term traumas and troubles
- Remove curses and banish pain, suffering, and negativity from your life
- And so much more…

Book of Shadows

A printable PDF to support you in your spiritual transformation.

Within the pages, you will find:
- Potion and tinctures tracking sheet
- Essential oils log pages
- Herbs log pages
- Magical rituals and spiritual body goals checklist
- Tarot reading spread sheets
- Weekly moon and planetary cycle tracker
- And so much more

Get all the resources for FREE by visiting the link below

https://dreamlifepress.com/four-free-gifts

Introduction

I once knew a guy who killed someone, but not in the way you're thinking.

Back in 2014, my friend David was on a standard airport run to meet another friend, Sarah, who was returning to the States after spending a year studying in Europe. He picked her up and dropped her off at her parent's home at around two o'clock in the morning. He then took the freeway home. While cruising down the empty road, his life changed in an instant.

Without warning, a hooded man ran in front of his car. Of course, being about 3 a.m. and pitch black except for the car headlights, there was zero time to react. The car slammed into the man, and David screamed out curses louder than he'd ever had in his life. He pulled over to the side, turned on the hazard lights, and instantly grabbed his phone to call the police. They arrived in minutes.

After spending hours and hours on high alert waiting for the police to conduct their investigation, including taking statements and administering alcohol and drugs tests (his tests ultimately came back clean), the man David hit was pronounced dead at the scene. After four hours, the freeway cleared, and the police gave David a lift home. At seven in the morning, David walked into his home with two police officers in tow. His worried girlfriend came downstairs to greet him, as he'd incredibly late and hadn't been answering calls. At the sight of the officers, her panic escalated.

Shocked and finally coming down from the adrenaline rush, David sat down and allowed the officers to inform his girlfriend what had happened and detail the next course of action. Tired, shocked, and panicked, David's girlfriend fainted, collapsing onto the tiled floor without warning. She hit her head hard, and as she bled from the wound, one of the officers called for an ambulance.

David proceeded to spend another six hours in the emergency room as doctors ran tests on his girlfriend before concluding she'd basically had a massive panic attack. The events of the night had been overwhelming for her. When they finally made their way back home, David slept for two days before experiencing his first-ever panic attack the moment he woke up - a feeling that convinced him, to this day, that he'd rather die.

The investigation was closed a few months later, and David faced no charges. Investigators discovered that the guy who'd run into the road had been severely depressed and addicted to drugs and alcohol. Texts and phone calls from that night revealed that his girlfriend had broken up with him, and while he may not have wanted to die, his blood alcohol content was miles past the legal limit.

David felt fine for a while, telling us that he'd had so many epiphanies from that night. For the first time, he saw that life was precious, and that anything could happen when you least expect it. He was grateful for his instincts; for controlling the car and safely pulling over to the side of the road. If he'd panicked or lost control, he could have easily lost his life that night. He was grateful he'd survived, but gutted that the man's loved ones had lost a brother, a son, and a friend.

However, three years later, David sunk into a deep depression. Gradually, he started spending less time with family and friends. He broke up with his girlfriend shortly after she moved away, and David quickly found himself in a toxic, controlling relationship. He drastically lost weight, stopped going to the gym, and frequently sat in the local park in the rain staring into the distance, seemingly disconnected from the world around him.

I would sit with him on these benches sometimes, and we'd talk about television shows or the news. I would tell him what our friends were up to or just talk about a movie I'd seen. He rarely spoke. He mostly stared at the ground when I was with him. One time, however, something changed. He turned to me, gripped my jacket as the rain poured, and stared me dead in the eyes. His words chilled me.

"I'm so scared, Layla. I'm scared I'm going to do something. I'm scared I'm going to hurt myself. I don't want to die, but there's a part of me that wants to. It's getting stronger."

I didn't reply. I pulled him into my arms and held him tight. He burst into tears. We cried together. David tells me that conversation was a turning point in his life. He became proactive. He started developing new habits, saw a professional therapist, and slowly made it to the other side. There's no denying he's come so far and I can happily say that his suicidal thoughts stopped. He's starting to really enjoy his life again as a happy and healthy individual.

That day was also a turning point in my life. Already deep into my self-development journey, I started to realize that there's a powerful and overwhelming power in our lives, yet most of the time we're unaware of its presence. I think for many of us, we're so used to this power being present and relentless that we don't know what it's like to live without it.

Of course, I'm talking about the voice in our heads.

David's was an extreme case. Having gone through such a traumatic and impactful experience, the voice in his head was louder than ever before, basically shouting and screaming so loudly that he could hear nothing else. It became all-consuming, and why he felt so lost and depressed.

Yet, this voice exists in all of us. The voice that tells you that you can't do something, so you don't. The voice that tells you a person doesn't like you, you said the wrong thing, you made a mistake, and now everybody hates you. The voice that declares that you're lonely, worthless, stressed, broke, stupid, not good enough, too fat or too thin, not pretty or handsome, or not successful enough.

The voice that goes on and on and on and never shuts up. And when you listen, you're devastated. When you don't, you still know, deep down, it's there in the shadows, and you're waiting for it to come back again. You feel it..

Overthinking is running rampant in our modern-day society. It's a pandemic that's been growing for decades, becoming more and more common, creating more of an impact than ever before. Rates of anxiety and depression are higher than ever before. Suicide rates are still growing year by year (it's the second leading cause of death of people aged 10-34), and more people agree that they aren't happy with the lives they are living.

A 2016 study found that only 31% of Americans say they are happy. Comparatively, 1 in 5 American adults will experience a mental health problem each year, 1 in 20 of those serious, and with 50% of all lifetime mental illnesses beginning at the age of 14 (75% by the age of 24), this is something that needs to be addressed. The voice in our heads bombards us every single day from the moment we're awake until the moment we fall asleep, and sometimes it keeps us awake.

I'm not talking about overthinking as a mental health problem. Have you ever wanted to write a book? Start a business? Have the friends you want? Follow your dream? Have healthy and happy relationships? Live the life you want to live? Chances are, you already know how the voice in your head is making you unhappy. It's the reason you were drawn to this book. You know your reasons, and now it's time to take action.

Before we continue, I want you to write down your reason for picking up this book. Whatever it is, write it down on a piece of paper right now and keep it beside you. Whatever anxious feelings or overthinking thoughts you have and how they are stopping you from being who you want to be, write it down.

You may be wondering why I told you David's story. It's a dark tale, but it's one with a light at the end of the tunnel. David was in a dark place, and I'm sure you know or have heard of someone in a similar position. People like David, like myself, and everyone who go on this journey, are living, breathing proof that you don't need to live in a world where the voice in your head is in control.

There are solutions. There are remedies. There are ways you can take back control of your life and keep yourself in check. And guess what? There are ways and things you can do that will help you achieve genuine happiness in your life. This is what we'll cover in this book—twenty-seven ways to stop overthinking, to calm the voice and the relentless thoughts, to stop worrying about things, and to stop feeling so stressed.

Twenty-seven ways to stay calm, find peace, and be happy.

So, take that piece of paper that you wrote the way that your internal voice is holding you back, tear it into tiny pieces or screw it up into a ball, and throw it in the bin. Today's the day the change starts, and your journey begins.

I'm ready when you are.

How to Use This Book

While there's no right or wrong way to use and learn from this book, I want to take time to remind you that this book doesn't need to be read linearly. To keep things easy, I've broken down the book into five easy chapters covering the following:

Chapter One is about understanding the problem. It's about figuring out why you overthink and how you got to where you are today.

Once we understand the problem, we can work out how to fix it and how to make things better.

Chapter Two is about dealing with stress. We all feel stress, whether it's caused by our overthinking or our stress leads to overthinking. When the voice makes itself heard, anxiety strikes, or if a situation isn't going your way, stress ensues, and if you don't know how to deal with it, it's going to take over. I will show you how to stop that from happening.

Chapter Three is about dealing with anxiety. I like to think of anxiety as long-term stress. Technically, they are different (we'll go into this later), but I think of stress as being an in-the-moment state of mind, whereas anxiety is how you're affected long-term by life and your own thoughts. It takes different strategies to cope with this way of living.

Chapter Four dives into the ways you can deal with overthinking in the moment, whether you've just started thinking about something or you're dealing with your habitual thinking patterns and self-talk. How you talk to yourself is everything in this world, and this chapter is about taking control from the uncontrollable. It's about truly grasping and becoming you.

Finally, we move onto Chapter Five, which is where we change course, moving away from dealing with problems, and instead basking in the joys of the solutions. Chapter Five is about physically rewiring your brain for happiness and learning the techniques and methods that will help you genuinely open the doors to living the life you want.

The methods detailed in the following chapters are based on psychology and science, and I'll link studies and references along the way. Basically, these are strategies that have been proven to work and deliver results. You just need to build the habits and implement them.

When I say this I mean choosing what works for you. While there are methods in these pages that won't resonate with you and you may not think will work, many more methods will change your life. Read this book however you want. If you see a method here that speaks to you and you want to find out more, then jump to that chapter and find out about it.

However, I highly recommend reading the book once through first, taking in all the information you can about each method, and then deciding how you want to proceed. You may be pleasantly surprised with some methods, and you may find a solution you never thought of. Nevertheless, the most important thing to remember is that you're here to figure out what works best for you as an individual, and only you can do that.

This book exists to provide you with options and knowledge to help you make an informed decision, the best for you. Okay, I think that's enough talking for now. Let's begin this journey.

Chapter One

Finding Your Foundations

Back when my overthinking and the state of my mental health were at their worst, I felt trapped and lost, believing these feelings were going to last forever. At least, that's what the voice was telling me. When you're not feeling okay, whether you're feeling mildly anxious, a bit panicky, or downright depressed, it's a strange phenomenon that we feel as though this is how our life will be from here on out.

Negative feelings tend to be all-consuming, meaning that you can't seem to see past them. Rational thought seems to disappear, and the more you overthink and go down the rabbit hole, the harder it seems to get out of it. There's a lot of talk claiming, "it's okay not to be okay," and while that's true, and everybody will certainly find themselves in dark places from time to time, it's important to remember that "it's not okay to not be okay" forever, and this will never be the case.

This book's main focus is on the concept of overthinking. This can be a standalone condition, where if you're feeling stressed or going through something, you overthink. It can just happen, sometimes randomly, and minutes or hours can pass, and you suddenly realize that your mind has been racing at a million thoughts a minute, preventing you from being happy in the moment.

Overthinking is also a symptom of mental health conditions like anxiety and depression. It's important to reiterate that this book will not help you overcome these conditions. Psychological conditions can vary dramatically in their nature and impact, sometimes based on life's circumstances and sometimes being a biological condition that requires medical help and treatment. Overthinking is a severe part of that, so while you'll need to address those issues separately, I do hope this book can help you on your path to recovery and stepping forward into a better, happier, more peacefully content life that you truly deserve—a life we *all* truly deserve.

It all starts with figuring out where you are on your own personal journey and working from there. "Figuring out where you are and what's going on with you?" I remember when I was told the same thing, and I couldn't think of anything worse than diving into my own problems and life situation. Does anyone really want to take a long look into that mirror? Probably not.

However, it's the first and most important step in every journey. It's the process of positioning yourself on your map so you can plot your route. And, of course, no one can tell you where you are because your life situation is your own, and nobody else knows you as you do. That being said, this chapter will help you find out where you're standing. So, let's dive into it.

Why Do We Overthink?

There are multiple reasons why you overthink. The most common is believing that there's something wrong with you. Hear me out, just because you overthink that doesn't mean there's something wrong with you. Overthinking is usually a symptom created from the long-term build-up of things happening in your life that has led you to where you mentally are right now. Chances are you've not been an overthinker your entire life, but it is rather a process that has gradually become more and more prominent to you.

Think of it this way. Let's imagine you were in a relationship with someone during your school or college years. You really liked this person, and you might even go as far as to say they were your first love or your childhood sweetheart. Everything was amazing, and you were happy. However, you found out your partner cheated on you, and you broke up and never spoke again.

During your grieving period, where you're effectively mourning the loss of your relationship, you think about what you did wrong. How could you have been better? What could you have done different to stop them from going off with someone else? Did you push them away? Let's face it, teenagers and young adults are never great at communication since this is the stage where we're all still learning how to do it properly, and chances are you're never going to get any answers.

Time passes, and you move on. You end up in another relationship, and you're happy. However, because of your past experiences, you start to think about what you could do differently and how you can make the other person happier because you don't want them to cheat on you. You start feeling anxious when they go out and see other people because you're scared of being cheated on. You imagine what the other person is doing and other dreadful fantasies. You prepare yourself to hear the news of them cheating on you, as though that's going to soften the blow when it happens.

Since you're not your genuine self, but rather are acting on emotions arising from your incessant overthinking, the relationship breaks down. Because of this, your overthinking goes into overdrive. What did you do wrong? What could you do better? Is it you? Were they the one? Will you ever find happiness? Thus, the overthinking becomes worse.

This process continuously snowballs throughout your life, in all areas of your life, until the problems are addressed. But you're not going to be able to address the problems if you can't deal with the overthinking in the first place, which is precisely what this book is about and aims to teach you how to do.

Another quick example: If you're working a job you hate, but you get fired or leave, and you end up going through similar experiences with multiple jobs, then you start overthinking when it comes to working and managing your career. This causes a degree of overthinking, which will typically cause more problems, and thus more overthinking. It's a continuous, self-sustaining cycle.

So yes, when asking what has caused your overthinking, it could be coming from you—not you as a person, but rather the series of events and experiences you've been a part of throughout your life. By learning the methods throughout this book, you should be able to break the cycle of overthinking so you can address the problems at their core.

Some other issues you may be experiencing in your life that can lead to overthinking include:

- Poor confidence or self-esteem
- Not believing in yourself or trusting your instincts
- You are protective of yourself or others
- Perfectionism
- Habitual thinking patterns

There are other external factors that trigger overthinking. The best and most recent example is the COVID-19 pandemic. Of course, a prominent and global event that received immense coverage on the Internet and on the news, usually 24-hours a day. With so much information about the death and destruction it's causing, how could you not overthink the pandemic?

Such an event causes panic and anxiety on a mass scale. Personally, I wasn't really worried about the pandemic. I knew people who got it and were ill, and I also knew several people who died from it. I tend to believe that when it's time to go, it's time, and while it's a tragedy for such a horrible situation to be our reality, I try to come to peace with it as much as possible.

However, when you're in bed at night, and you get a slight cough, you feel like you should be able to smell something but you can't, or you're feeling just slightly off, of course, after so much news and media coverage, you're going to think *Oh my god, I've caught it, and now I'm going to be ill, and I could even die*. If you let these thoughts continue unchecked, that's a serious rabbit hole you'll fall into.

With that, it's easy to see that external factors can play a huge role when it comes to the reason why you overthink.

How Our Brains are Designed to Overthink

That's right. Sometimes, there's nothing wrong with you, no life situations going on, and no external issues that could cause you to overthink. In truth, our brains are hardwired by our fundamental human nature to overthink. Not in the relentless way that some of us do, but there is undoubtedly an element of thinking that is hardwired into us for survival instincts.

This is simply how it works. Your mind is not who you are. This might be easily understandable, or it may go over your head, but hear me out. You are not your thoughts. Your brain is as much a part of you as your arm or leg is. Your brain is a tool. It's meant to solve problems, just like your hand is a tool for picking things up and touch. Just like your eyes help you see the world.

Your brain is a tool to help you solve problems and to overcome issues with the primary goal of keeping you alive. When you're feeling hungry, it releases hormones that make you want to eat. When you eat, it rewards you with dopamine to make you feel good for fulfilling a need, thus keeping your body in excellent working order.

Back in the days of cavemen and surviving in challenging conditions, our human brain excelled because it could solve problems that kept us alive even during the harshest of environments and situations. We still have the same brain that works in the same way. It's an advanced thinking computer system that aims to keep us alive. Note, this doesn't mean that our mind exists to make us happy. It literally aims to keep us alive without any considerations for our emotions.

However, we live in a very different world from the one our ancestors did hundreds of years ago. While the world isn't perfect, most of us have our basic needs taken care of, and we live in relative comfort. This means our brainpower is spent on other things, like worrying if we're acceptable based on the number of likes we have on social media, whether our football team is winning, we're getting enough sleep, we're too fat or too thin, wear the right clothes, have enough money, are making the most of our lives before we die, or living in the moment, and so on. You get the idea.

There are so many stimuli in our day-to-day lives, far more than there were thousands of years ago, that our brain is now hooked on thinking about all of it, which is why it can feel like you're constantly and relentlessly thinking all day every day. Understanding that this is happening to you is the first step in realizing what it is causing you to overthink. You can then use the many methods outlined in this book to reduce your overthinking habits, putting yourself in a position to take back control of your life, whether that means being more aware of your overthinking triggers, limiting your stimuli, or just figuring out what in life is important to you, and basically reducing your life down to what is essential to you.

An obvious example of this happening in my own life is my

relationship with writing. This was especially the case when I was starting out and attempting to write my first books. I had a perfectionist mindset where I needed to word every sentence and take every word choice to court to decide whether it was good enough or not. I obsessed over whether people would get value from what I wrote, whether I was wasting my time, or how I would take the criticisms that would inevitably come from my readers.

However, my overthinking became so much that it ended up holding me back because I was so focused on everything else except what was necessary, in this case, writing. Now, you may be thinking that worrying about writing a book and trying to deal with how it's being taken could be a big deal. After all, no one wants to write a book and be hated because of it.

The point is that these worries are caused, created, and sustained by the same biological programming in our minds that we had thousands of years ago when it came to surviving. Basically, we see everyday situations in our own lives, and our mind treats them as life-or-death situations. A panic attack is the body's fight-or-flight system kicking in. Whereas it used to kick in when faced with a bear or saber-toothed tiger, for obvious reasons, it's now kicking in when we don't get as many likes on Instagram as we usually get.

This may feel ridiculous to you, but part of survival is being accepted as part of the tribe and the rest of humanity. In the past, if you were living in the woods on your own and you got ill, you were going to die. If you get ill or sick when you're living in the tribe and everybody looks after each other, then you're more likely to live and thrive since you're taken care of and provided for. This has created a biological need to be accepted by our peers, an instinct that is hardwired into our brains. This is why it still hurts when you receive negative comments from strangers online, and it can take such a negative toll on your wellbeing, your mental and physical health.

What Happens When You Overthink?

We've talked a lot about where overthinking comes from, and you may be wondering why this is a problem. After all, if you didn't think, nothing would get done. You couldn't have ideas, have connected relationships, or solve the problems in your life. You would just be a naive shell of a person wandering from situation to situation without much going on.

We even spoke about how thinking and analyzing situations is an integrated part of your human instinct that is necessary for your survival. How can this all be bad?

Well, just like we spoke briefly about in the introduction, thinking about something is fine. Incessantly thinking about something is not. With my writing, overthinking was holding me back. In a relationship where you may be dealing with trust issues, overthinking will stop you from connecting with your partners fully and therefore stop you from developing a healthy relationship. It's all very situation-dependent, but the problems and consequences of overthinking, unfortunately, go far deeper than just that.

From a happiness standpoint, you can't be happy if you're overthinking. To overthink is to be in survival mode and to try and figure out a problem. If you want, remember that to overthink is to believe there is a problem in your life that needs solving. It's the very idea of being discontent. You want to be somewhere you're not currently, or you want some specific detail or situation in your life to be different.

Imagine you're on vacation, and you're relaxing on the beach and watching the world go by. You turn to your partner, and they look amazing in the sunset. Are you thinking at this moment? Are you worried about bills or your career? Are you stressed about anything? Of course not. Even if those feelings of peace only last several seconds. It's that content feeling of peace that keeps you happy in the moment.

You can find moments like this in all areas of your life, in any situation, sometimes randomly and without reason. It goes without saying, you're not going to find the opportunity to be happy and peaceful if your mind is constantly racing. This book aims to create more opportunities for that space to appear, and therefore more chances to be happy.

Finally, there are the physical effects of overthinking.

While it's true that overthinking is not a medical term and it's classed as a medical condition in itself, there's plenty of research that proves it's a problem and jeopardizes for your mental and physical health. For example, Ashley Carroll, a psychologist working at the Parkland Memorial Hospital, states:

"When it becomes destructive to our life or really impairs our daily functioning, for example, if you're having trouble sleeping at night because you can't turn these thoughts off, that's impacting your daily functioning." She goes on to explain how it can affect your appetite. It may cause you to isolate yourself from other people. It can cause stress and increase existing stress levels by physically raising the levels of cortisol (the stress hormone) in your body. Excessive amounts of this hormone, over longer periods of time, can lead to other health problems like:

- weight gain, mostly around the midsection and upper back
- rounding of the face
- acne & poor-quality skin
- slowed healing after injury
- muscle weakness
- severe fatigue
- irritability
- difficulty concentrating
- high blood pressure
- headache

In turn, prolonged and unmanaged exposure to these conditions can lead to cardiovascular disease, osteoporosis, diabetes, and even psychiatric disorders. Sure, these are problems in extreme cases, and the issues aren't direct, but I'm sure I speak for everyone when I say you're going to want to avoid both the long and short-term risks of overthinking and everything that accompanies these issues.

To cut a long story short, you're going to want to focus on decluttering your mind and opening yourself up to a new way of living. I'm not denying that thinking is a good thing, and you're going to need to think things through from time to time. However, excessive thinking, ruminating, and allowing your thoughts to control your mind and prevent you from living in the *now* is a problem, and I'm sure these last two chapters have brought these issues to mind and are motivating you to make a change.

I think by this point in the book, you get the idea. Overthinking equals bad. Focused, productive thinking, peace, and happiness equals good. Now, we dive into the methods for dealing with these issues, and this is going to take up the rest of the book. If you're ready to start a new chapter of your life while putting the shackles of overthinking behind you, turn the page and take your first step.

Chapter Two

Methods for Managing Stress

Overthinking and stress go hand in hand. I'm sure you don't need any examples to know this is the case. Think about when something terrible has happened to you and how you've felt during and afterward. Let's say you've lost your job. You get stressed and start thinking about what you're going to do, where you're going to find another job, how you'll pay the bills, what your partner will say, and how you're going to afford your rent. The list goes on and on.

You get stressed, start overthinking, get more stressed, and the cycle continues. The first strategy is how to deal with this stress when it arises. These are short-term fixes that can help you stay grounded and in control of your thinking. It's about catching yourself getting stressed, implementing one of these techniques, and getting yourself back under control, all while minimizing the risk of feeling anxious and overthinking.

That's not to say you won't think. If you lose your job, you're not just going to do some deep-breathing exercises and suddenly forget it ever happened. Of course not, you're human. The idea is to reduce the stress and heightened emotions so you can think clearly and concisely to find a solution. It's all about thinking with purpose instead of getting caught up in the relentless worrying and anxiety.

If you're feeling stressed, these are the methods you're going to want under your belt.

Method 1

The 5-4-3-2-1 Grounding Technique

The 5-4-3 Grounding Technique is one of the most popular anxiety-reducing techniques and is taught by professionals, counselors, therapists, and behavioral experts worldwide. It doesn't matter what situation you find yourself in - if you catch yourself experiencing heightened emotions that feel out of control, this is a method that will help you regain focus, stay grounded, and find peace in the otherwise all-consuming storm of thought and feeling.

The strategy is simple. You start by paying attention to what you're feelings. Are you stressed? Anxious? Upset? Are you about to do something nerve-racking, like attend a job interview, speak publicly, or ask someone out? How do you feel? Tense? Worried? On edge? On the verge of a panic attack?

You don't need to do anything with these feelings but pay attention to them and acknowledge their existence. One of the biggest problems we have in life is realizing that we're not feeling 100% and then running away from those feelings because we *should* feel okay and *should* manage what we're going through. Dismissing these feelings is one of the worst things you can do because it invalidates how you feel and will only make your anxiety worse. It says that what you're feeling is *not allowed* and *bad*, leading to focusing what could be wrong with you.

This isn't the case. If you're asking someone out on a date, applying for the job of your dreams, or doing anything that matters to you, no matter how big or small, you're going to feel nervous or excited because it's perfectly natural.

All you need to do is take several deep breaths. Inhale through your nose, filling your chest up with as much air as you possibly can, and then exhale very slowly and steadily through your mouth. Repeat this several times and just sit with your feelings. You don't need to do anything but sit and be still. Focus on your breathing. If your mind starts to wander, and you notice yourself getting caught up in random thoughts, just bring your attention back to your breathing. Even if you do this every few seconds, that's fine. It's just part of the learning process.

After you've done the breathing exercise, keep breathing steadily, but move onto the 5-4-3 aspect of this technique. It goes as follows.

Five. Look around you and mentally note five things you can see. These can be anything, from a ceiling light, fan, a pen on your desk, a phone, a person, or a tree. Just look around and mentally note five things in your surroundings.

Four. Bring your awareness a little closer to your personal space, and name four different things you can touch. This could be something as simple as your pocket, your shirt, or your chair. Try to make these things different from the things you can see.

Three. Now switch senses and list three things you can hear. Listen for a car, bird, or people having a conversation. Ideally, you want to choose things that are outside your body and in your surroundings, but if you can hear and notice your own footsteps, that's perfectly fine.

Two. Now move to your nose and try to find two things you can actively smell. Can you smell coffee? Printer ink? Food? The smell of the city? A person or their fragrance? If you need to, take a walk and list what you can smell.

One. The final part is to take note what you can taste. What does the inside of your mouth taste like? Gum? Coffee? Did you have a mint? If you can't taste anything, take a moment to eat or drink something and pay attention to the details of what you're consuming.

This method may seem basic, but it's one of the most powerful behavioral techniques in the world. When you're stressed and overthinking, your attention is internalized. You're focusing on the tense feelings and rapid succession of thoughts, unable to pay attention to the outside world. When someone is feeling sad, they may end up just sitting and staring out into space. They have zero awareness of the world outside of their thoughts.

In my own experiences, I used to have panic attacks where I got tunnel vision. It was as though the edges of my vision were turning black, so I could only see this blurry haze in front of me. Nothing was in focus, and I couldn't pay attention to anything. When I lived at home, I used to ask my parents to tell me a story about anything just to take my mind off the worry and racing thoughts, and they would, but rarely would I hear anything they were saying.

Using this technique made it possible for me to detach myself from those rabbit hole feelings in a simple way that didn't require a lot of effort but was still enough to calm my mind and get me out of internalized thinking cycles. For me, by the time I got to Four or Three, I was already starting to calm down and see the world around me. The more I practiced this, the easier it became.

It is best to practice this technique when you're not feeling anxious. Just go through the steps once a day to really embed what you're doing and to make it easier to know what you're doing. You also want to make sure you're listing the items out loud, or clearly in your head. This will help you acknowledge what you're seeing and experiencing, increasing the benefits the method provides.

Finally, make sure you're keeping your eyes open, and if you're really struggling, then get a friend to help. You may find it much easier to go through the steps, especially at first, with a friend, and the interaction with them alone can help you ground you. Once you've reached the end of the steps, your stress levels may be a lot lower than when you started.

METHOD 2

Deep Breathing Away the Stress

Deep breathing is one of the most straightforward, yet powerful, stress-reducing techniques in the world and has been practiced for thousands of years. There's a reason why you have an image in your head of someone meditating and deep breathing when they're feeling stressed and need to calm down. Breathing through stress is practically common knowledge, yet so few people will take the time to learn how to do it properly to enjoy its benefits.

What's more, this method of stress reduction is backed by science and has been for decades. A 2007 study into stress management techniques for nurses, while detailing how stress affects their productivity levels and career retention rates, found that adding three- to five-minute deep breathing sessions into their agenda meetings radically improved the nurse's productivity levels, happiness levels, and general wellbeing.

Sticking with medical personnel, a two-year study following medical academics and students published in 2007 concluded that:

"The Deep Breathing Meditation technique was successfully implemented each academic year, and it provided students with a promising solution for meeting challenging academic and professional situations."

In fact, if you search *deep breathing studies* in the Google Scholar platform (a database/search engine for finding academic studies), you'll receive over 27,000 results. That's how powerful and well-researched this process is. And it still blows my mind that this is something you don't need any tools to practice. You simply stop what you're doing, take a time out, and breathe.

So, how do you do it?

The most common technique is known as *belly breathing*. You can do this any time, even when you're not feeling particularly stressed, and you'll find that it makes you feel very calm and very centered, enabling you to think more clearly and more concisely. It improves your general focus, and generally makes you feel more peaceful. Here are the steps:

- Sit with your back is straight in the chair or lie flat. It is important to remember that you need to be in a comfortable position that you can hold for the next few minutes without having to move around.

- Place your right hand on your stomach near your diaphragm - between your ribs and your stomach. Place your other hand flat on your chest.

- Take a deep inhale through your nose and expand your stomach as you breathe. With your hand, feel the air filling your lungs and expanding your body. However, make sure you try and keep your chest as flat and as still as possible.

- Once your lungs are full, and you feel as though you can't take any more air in, press your lips together as though you're whistling and push all the air out slowly and steadily. Try to keep the breathing as consistent as possible and keep the speed the same from start to finish, as much as you can. Take your time. There's no need to rush.

- Repeat this process between three and ten times. Remember not to rush this process. It's easy to fall into the trap of trying to rush through the breathing exercises as quickly as possible, as though getting to the end will make you feel better, quicker. This is not the case. It's the process of breathing slowly that will help relax your frantic mind.

The Belly Breathing method above is undoubtedly the easiest breathing exercise you can practice because you can practice anytime, anywhere, and you don't need to master any special techniques. You just breathe and control the depth and the speed of said breaths. However, there are more advanced breathing techniques that could be more effective for you. All you need to do is try them all to see which works best for you.

The first advanced method is known as the 4-7-8 method. It's pretty much the same as belly breathing and can be performed either sitting or lying down. Simply adopt the same position as the belly breathing technique, counting to four seconds as you inhale. You want your breath from start to finish to be four seconds long. It can take a bit of practice to get this right, but it can be so effective once you've mastered it, so surely practice outside of feeling stressed.

Once you've inhaled, hold your breath for seven seconds. Just hold and count in your head. When the seven seconds are up, exhale out your mouth (the same technique as belly breathing), but make the exhale lasts for eight seconds. Repeat this process three to seven times, or until you fee; calmer. Personally, I feel calmer after one round of these breaths, so try it out for yourself and you'll understand what I mean.

There are other breathing practices you can try as well, such as developing a morning breathing routine or roll breathing, but these are only advised once you have practiced the other techniques because it's easy to feel dizzy if you're new to the practice. Just remember to take your time and learn at your own pace. Don't rush to stand up after your breathing practice, and just listen to your body.

However, it is important to remember, regardless of what practice you're doing, to take note of how you feel after the breathing practice is over. Take a moment or two to reflect on how you feel compared to how you felt when you started. Do you feel calmer? Do you feel less stressed? Do you feel relaxed and peaceful? Is there any change at all?

No matter what you feel, it's essential to acknowledge the existence of those feelings, to validate them, and to accept them for what they are. In my own experience, I've felt at least a little calmer and more grounded 95% of the time, and the other 5% of the time, at least my thoughts have calmed, and I'm able to think more clearly and with purpose, rather than just trying to get caught up with my racing mind.

Getting to this point is a massive improvement when it comes to overcoming your overthinking tendencies and taking back control.

METHOD 3

Understand the Causes of Your Stress

At this point, you have two or three ways of dealing with stress when you're lost in the moment. There are other techniques you can use, including simple ones like squeezing a stress ball or removing yourself from the situation you're in and going for a short walk to clear your mind. However, the methods mentioned are those proven capable of helping lessen your stress levels.

That's not to say things are going to be perfect. There are still going to be times where you get stressed and lose yourself in your thoughts. Nobody is perfect. There will be good times and bad times. The trick is to try and reduce that stress as much as you can, individually, without comparing yourself with anybody else. The more you practice, the better you get. However, these techniques are short-term solutions to a long-term problem.

You'll start moving towards a positive, peaceful, and happier life once you start identifying your stress sources and doing what you can to remove them. In all aspects of life, prevention is always better than cure, and if you can stop something bad from happening, in other words stopping yourself from becoming stressed in the first place.

However, there are no easy fixes. You can't just click your fingers and the stress disappears. As time goes on and your life changes, stress factors will come and go. Some are big. Some are small. It's not the stress factor that's the problem, it's how you deal with it that matters.

So, where do you start? Get yourself a pen and paper as you make your way through this, and let's find out.

First, there will be stress factors that you know are there and don't need explanation. In my early 20s, I was a little dumb and took out a loan I couldn't afford. When I missed a payment and was imposed interest that made the payments ridiculous, I felt incredibly stressed. I didn't need anyone to tell me that my financial stress was a serious problem in my life. Of course, this isn't a problem that can be solved overnight.

The important thing for me to remember was that I had a problem, and I needed to work on solutions. This meant cutting back on subscriptions, saving money where I could, and paying off the debt in larger chunks. I took on some overtime hours at work and worked hard for months until I was able to clear my debt and finally free myself from the stress.

Some examples of prominent stress sources in our lives include:

- Financial issues
- Health problems (physical and mental)
- Problems or conflicts at work

- Conflicts in your family or friendships

- Losing loved ones

- Losing your job

- Suffering from an injury

- Losing something you care about

- Arguing with a friend

These are all valid reasons to feel stress, and you know that these things stress you out. If you're feeling stressed about any of these things or anything that's happening in your own life, take some deep breaths and remember, these situations and their effects don't last forever. Everything is temporary. Most of these issues are short-term (even if it means that the problem lasts for a few months, that's still temporary), and using the short-term methods to relieve the stress is a good approach.

However, there will be other situations where the sources of stress are not so obvious, and you need to be proactive in your life when it comes to figuring these out. If you're not aware that something is making you feel stressed, how are you ever going to do anything about it?

The first step to finding the problem is looking for the signs. Even just reading this chapter will massively help when it comes to figuring out when things are not as they should be, so open your mind and let the following information sink in.

Stress will manifest itself in your life in different ways, but there will always be a sign. These could be physical or mental. You may feel:

- Pain somewhere in your body
- Headaches
- Tension in your muscles
- Digestive problems like constipation or nausea
- Excessive period pains
- Missed periods
- A change in your sex drive
- Increased heart rate
- Restlessness
- Insomnia and troubles sleeping
- Other changes in sleeping patterns
- Changes in your diet or appetite
- Lack of motivation
- Increase in bad habits or escapism (such as binging food or television)
- Increased or heightened emotions
- Lack of concentration

If you feel different from how you usually feel, this typically means that something is bothering you, and you need to zero in on how you're feeling and why. Sometimes you may be in a situation where you feel stressed. After an argument, you may feel a rush of adrenaline and anger, and it's obvious why you feel that way.

On the other hand, someone might irritate you in little ways that compound as days and weeks go by. You may not notice the little bits of stress building up, but after a few weeks you may feel stressed out, and you're not sure why.

The trick is to keep an eye out for the symptoms. The more you do this, the more you'll recognize your own individual signs of stress. Everyone is different, and stress affects us in different ways. Once you've noticed the signs and you know you're stressed, it's time to figure out why.

Pay attention to when you feel your stress symptoms, and you'll quickly see what's bringing you stress. This requires a certain degree of self-awareness and mindfulness, but if you keep paying more attention to your thoughts and how you're feeling throughout the day, you can start to pin down what's causing you stress.

To summarize all this, this method is simple and concise. From the beginning, write down what causes you stress. Now write down how you feel when you think about those subjects or get stressed about them. Then think about other areas in your life when you feel the same stress symptoms and try to figure out why you're feeling that way.

Are you experiencing conflict? Do you need to say something? Do you want to express yourself? I was recently talking to my friend

Nicole about her being a bridesmaid at her friend's wedding. She was excited, but something seemed off. I asked her about it, and she said she didn't know why, but she felt weird about going to the wedding. She asked for my advice, and I told her the same thing I'm telling you.

I told her to go home and write down what she feels when she is stressed. To write down the things in her life that she knows brings her stress, and how she feels. Then I told her to pay attention to when she had the same feelings in other areas of her life and to write down when she felt this way and what she was thinking about.

After a week of trying this method, she soon realized that she was getting stressed over her position in life. All her friends were getting promotions, starting families, and getting married, but she had none of those, and felt like she was falling behind, wasn't successful, and basically wasn't where she wanted to be. Becoming aware of this, she started practicing gratitude journaling and felt inspired to set out and do something she always dreamed of doing, which was opening an art gallery, which held its first exhibition last week.

Not all aspects of stress can be eliminated—far from it. You can't deal with or solve everything, nor can you be in a state of life where you're never going to feel stress again. What you can do is bring awareness to what causes you stress and take action, whether by reducing exposure, adjusting your perspective, or solving the problem. Less stress means less overthinking.

Method 4

Keeping a Stress Journal

Together with the method above, another fantastic way of monitoring when, where, and how you get stressed is to keep a stress journal, which can also be referred to as a stress diary. You've probably heard of the benefits of keeping a journal or diary before, especially if you have some experience in the self-help industry. It's one of the most talked-about lifestyle habits, and for good reason.

Some of the benefits you'll enjoy include:

- Reduced anxiety and depression
- The ability to clarify and focus on your goals
- Improving mindfulness
- Improves your IQ
- Helps you reflect, accept, and move on from past events
- Helps your injuries heal faster (yes, a medical study in New Zealand proved this!)

- Can strengthen your immune system
- Helps you learn from your experiences and grow
- Improves your communication skills
- Improves your quality of sleep
- Improves your memory capabilities
- Helps you plan and achieve your goals
- Helps you become happier and improves your mood
- Helps you solve problems in your life

Basically, the list goes on and on. Some of them may, admittedly, look strange. Can journaling really improve how well your immune system functions? Actually, yes. James Pennebaker, a psychologist, found that the act of journaling physically helps to strengthen immune system cells known as T-lymphocytes. The more aware of your life events you are, the less stress you have, meaning the less cortisol you'll have, which ultimately means your body can work at a higher standard. It's kind of crazy how much of a positive effect a simple habit can have.

Even though I say *simple habit*, anyone who has ever tried journaling knows it's not as easy to form the habit as it seems. A bad or busy day, a dull day where there's nothing to write, or a simple lack of energy before you go to sleep, can mean you miss a day of writing, then two, then three, and so on. In my own experience, even though I know about the benefits, journaling seems like one of the hardest habits to form, and I can easily let days go by without writing anything.

Over the years, I've come to learn that there's a core reason for this, and it's quite simple. My journaling efforts lacked direction. Because I was sitting down every day without a plan, hoping to write down what I had been up to and how I was feeling, on the days where not much happened, or I simply didn't feel like writing (which are the days where you'll get the most benefit if you do pick up a pen) were the easiest to miss.

However, when I changed my perspective on journaling and set a goal to write about something specific, everything changed, and the habit quickly fell into place. This is why it's so important for your goals to be crisp, clear, and concise. The more detailed your plan is (even if it changes along the way), the more likely you are to carry it out because you have a direction mapped out.

To keep this line of thought relevant to this book, it's time to start your own stress journal. Here's how to make it work for you.

First, get yourself a medium for writing. I recommend getting yourself a nice, dedicated notebook to write in because this is a space that can be used to know yourself and understand how your mind works. However, if writing by hand is not for you, there's no reason you can't use a computer. My personal preference is using the premium version of Diarly app, but a Word document can work if you're happy with that.

I would steer away from using your phone because it's far too easy to get distracted by notifications when you're writing, and it's no use if you're trying to write and keep finding yourself subjected to the pull of social media or the internet. If you have the discipline or prefer using a diary app (there are many good ones on your preferred app store), you're more than welcome to use one. Again, it's all about finding what works for you.

Now that you've got your writing space, you want to think about when you're going to write. It's highly recommended that you pick a good time that you can sit down and write in your journal every day since this will provide the most benefits and can help you form the habit. To randomly say you're going to write every day is nowhere near concise enough. Remember, the clearer and more concise you can be with your goals, the more likely you will make it work.

So, pick a time that works for you and try to stick to it as much as possible. Ideally, you're going to want to journal at the end of the day because you'll be able to reflect on everything that's happened while it's fresh in your mind and the feelings are present, something you wouldn't be able to do the following day. Again, it depends on you and your life. If you're busy in the evenings, then feel free to do it earlier.

Now comes the fun bit. Writing. Start by writing a little summary of your day and any significant events. If something stressful happened, take the time to write more about it. Write about the situation and why it made you feel stressed. Write about the feelings that came up, the bad part of the situation, and anything good about it. Write about potential solutions or hard feelings you may have. Write down whatever comes to mind, but don't judge what you write. Even if you wished the worst on someone because they screwed you over, just write it down and vent it out. Remember, your diary is your safe space to honestly express your thoughts and feelings.

Try to write for five minutes if you can, but write for as long as you want, just don't feel forced to keep going. If you start worrying about what to write and not expressing yourself appropriately, this is another form of overthinking. There's no right or wrong way to go about this, so remind yourself that there's no need to stress. Just write until you're satisfied and leave it at that.

That's really all you need to do. The benefits of keeping this diary lies in the act of writing. Jotting down your thoughts and feelings will give you a lot of clarity and a high level of reflection that you would otherwise be unable to get.

The problem with overthinking is that the thoughts in your mind aren't organized, so they rattle around and around, finding new points and returning to old ones, and it just keeps going. Writing the thoughts gives them structure and allows you to get them out of your head, enabling you to let them go.

If you're still unsure about this method, take a moment to try it now. Think about a problem in your life that you're thinking about and simply write ten bullet points on the subject. The bullet points can be anything—thoughts, feelings, details. It really doesn't matter. Just aim for ten bullet points, write them out, and see how you feel. I assure you that will be your proof.

METHOD 5

Mastering Autogenic Training

So far, the methods we've explored have been quite self-explanatory and straightforward. They are basic methods to help you overcome stress. But now that you've got your foundation, I think you're ready to try something a little more advanced - Autogenic Training.

This is a specialist technique whose sole aim is to promote feelings of calm and relaxation within you, no matter what's going on around you. When you're feeling the intensities of stress, anxiety, and overthinking, this is a great tool to have by your side and call upon when you need it. Neuropsychologists and related professionals recommend it as a great way to deal with overwhelming emotions, specifically stress, sadness, and frustration.

Developed in the 1920s, the technique is most commonly used by people undergoing CBT (Cognitive Behavioral Therapy), but it can be used as a standalone behavioral tool if needed. Scientifically, this technique has been proven to work. Most notably, a 2008 review of multiple studies *(Relaxation training for anxiety: a ten-years systematic review with meta-analysis)* found that autogenic training was highly effective at reducing anxiety symptoms and was recommended for reducing daily stress and coping with panic attacks, all of which are connected to overthinking.

There are other proven benefits as well, mainly those that come as side effects from people partaking in the practice and from personal experiences. These benefits include things like greater and increased self-esteem and self-confidence. People actively report being able to handle more stress and can stay focused and collected during stressful situations. Most people claim to generally feel more positive throughout their day-to-day life.

With the benefits of the practice clear and proven, let's jump into its practice. While the format can vary from person to person, the method below is generally considered the baseline.

First, make sure you're in a comfortable and relaxed position, either sitting down, lying on your back, or reclined. It doesn't really matter which you do; what matters is that you are comfortable and can sit for a few minutes without the urge to try and get more comfortable.

Close your eyes, take some deep breaths as we've already discussed, and then add some verbal cues. Ideally, you'll want to say them concisely and calmly - out loud or have someone say them to you. However, if you're in a position where you need to be a little quiet, saying them in your head is okay.

The list of cues may be as follows:

- I am completely calm (say once).

- My left arm is heavy (say six times).

- I am calm (say once).

- My right arm is warm (say six times).
- I am completely calm (say once).
- My heart beats calmly yet with purpose (say six times).
- I am entirely calm (say once).
- My breathing is calm and regular (say six times).
- I am completely calm (say once).

Of course, you can alter the cues to say whatever you want. If you tend to feel stress, for example, in your shoulders, then you can replace the right arm with your shoulder, drawing your focus to that area. You can also add on as many areas as you want and can go on for as long as you want. If you want to do a full-body scan, start with your head and move down to your toes.

Most commonly, someone might say, "Your arms are firm and grounded, breathe deeply, and open your eyes," and this would draw your practice to a close, helping you return to the *real world* in a grounded and peaceful state of mind. This kind of practice is all about bringing calm and peace into your life, especially when you feel like your overthinking or stress is all-consuming.

To give you an idea of just how powerful this repetitive practice is, it's most commonly used to treat those suffering from panic attacks, live with chronic pain diseases or conditions, have heart palpitations, or people living with phobias. The more you practice autogenic training, the more effective and beneficial the results become, all because you're actively training your brain to focus on these intentions. You're training yourself to be calmer and more peaceful, which is precisely what the practice achieves.

It's completely safe. Just take it at your own pace, or if you get the opportunity to, go through it with a professional or trained therapist who will be able to guide you through the process while teaching you the skills to do it for yourself in the future.

Method 6

How to Get Focused and Avoid Procrastination

For me, one of the biggest downfalls of feeling stressed is procrastination. I'm a sucker for escapism, so when I'm feeling stressed out, or I find myself constantly overthinking, which is usually linked to negative emotions like fear or sadness, I do everything I can not to think. This may mean binging Netflix or YouTube, playing video games, sleeping all the time, or eating a ton of junk food.

Because of the time I spend escaping through these activities, I don't get much work done during these harder times, and that makes me more stressed, which makes me procrastinate more, and it can end up being a vicious cycle that becomes harder and harder to break. However, it's not impossible to break once you know the tricks, tips, and strategies to get you back on track.

Of course, it would be effortless to write an entire book on this subject alone, but I'm going to break down this topic into just a few actionable points that have worked for me in the past and have allowed me to get back on track. Once I'm back on track, I'm focused and getting things done, which means less stress, less overthinking, and overall, more happiness and peace within myself.

There's no denying that this problem of being unable to focus, succumbing to excessive overthinking, consequently procrastination, and the stress and negative emotions was a big part of my life and held me back massively. This might be the case in your life, perhaps with varying effects. Here's a few tips on how to deal with this issue:

Making the Small Changes

Start by looking at your foundations - where you are right now. So, take a long look in the mirror. What's holding you back? When are you getting distracted, and what's bringing it on? You might find the distractions are obvious, and some are not. For example, if you're working at a desk and you have your phone with you, do you find yourself constantly picking it up and scrolling for a bit, going back to work, picking it up again, and so on?

Then you know your phone is a distraction. Ask yourself why you're picking it up. For me, one of the worst times was when I broke up with my ex-boyfriend, and being a little attached, I would pick up my phone to check if he was online, had posted something on Instagram, or was active. I know, attached is an understatement, something I've thankfully sorted out through counseling, but that hasn't stopped technology from being a distraction in other areas of my life.

Basically, think about how often you pick up your phone, watch TV, or check your emails when you know you should be doing something else. This is such a problem in the modern world because it's so easy.

It's so easy to pick up your phone, tap an app and get scrolling. It's harder to sit down and do the work. It's a lot harder to sit down and face what stresses or issues you're going through right now than it is to watch Netflix, which is why you're overthinking. Your brain is trying to figure out the problems in your life when it has the chance because you're not dummying it with content and interactive media.

That brings us back to this first point. You need to create a space in your life where you are free from distractions. This can be as simple as leaving your phone in another room, installing a website blocker, or locking your TV remote in a cupboard. No matter what your distraction is, the trick to remember is to put extra steps in your way to stop you from getting distracted. When you leave your phone in another room, you may instinctively reach out for it even though it's not with you (I still do all this time), but realize you've left it in the other room. Chances are you can't be bothered to go and get it, so you won't. Instead, you just carry on with whatever it was you should be doing.

This strategy is about minimizing distractions which ultimately minimize the risks of you finding something else to do instead of focusing on what you need to get done.

Getting Organized & Focused

One of the biggest problems I came across when trying to stay focused didn't stem from stress or overwhelming workloads, which surprised me. The main problem was the fact I wasn't organized. My workflow structure (to use a technical term) was all over the place, and I wasn't managing my time well. Because it felt like I was getting nothing done and my to-do list was always building up, I got stressed. So, I would take it out on myself or other people, and my overthinking became incessant, whether I was thinking about how much of a failure I was, how past my deadline I was going to be, what my boss was going to say, what my partner thought about me working all the time, and so on. I wasn't in a great place mentally.

Instead of being stuck in that loop, I learned how to get organized, manage my time well, and get stuff done, basically allowing me to master the management of my day-to-day life, releasing stress, boosting productivity, and finding peace. And don't believe these tips only apply to traditional workplace workflow. If you're a busy student, a frantic parent, starting a new project or hobby for yourself, or just trying to catch up on a busy day, these are strategies that will help you tenfold.

First, write a list. On your phone, PC, or a scrap of paper, it really doesn't matter. Write down everything you can think of that you need to do, even the small stuff that you don't think needs writing down, like charging your phone, getting lunch, or making a phone call. These small *micro* tasks are the most important. Write them all down in any order.

Now go through the list and highlight the three most important tasks you need to get done that day. No matter what, these are the tasks you'll be working on first. Make sure you label the tasks one, two, and three, in the order of their importance. As you go through your day, you'll do the first task, and because you know what you're doing, you remove the thinking aspect from your workflow. You just look at your list and know what you need to be doing without overthinking or stressing out.

When you've completed the first task, move on to the second, then the third. If you manage to get anything else done during the day, that's a bonus, and it's undoubtedly going to make you feel good, thanks to the dopamine release you get from smashing through your to-do list. If you have time-sensitive little jobs you need to do in the meantime, like making a phone call or picking your kids up from school, put it on the list and make it a part of your day's schedule.

Even if you're working on one project that's going to take all day or weeks, you need to break down the task into simple steps that you can cross off. For example, writing a book, a task that can take several months, can be broken down as follows:

- Get stationery and computer setup
- Activate distraction website blocker
- Put your phone in the other room
- Find a writing playlist that lasts six hours
- Get coffee and minimize other distractions
- Write the outline
- Write an introduction
- Write chapter summaries
- Write chapter one
- Write chapter two…

- ...Write conclusion

- Reread and hard edit

- Another hard edit

- Find beta readers

- And so on

The list above is one that would stretch over several months, and on a day-by-day basis, you'd break it down even further. Say you were writing chapter one in one day, your to-do list could be:

- Have breakfast

- Write from 9 - 12

- Have lunch

- Take the dog for a walk

- Write from 1:30 - 3

- Pick kids up

- Clean house

- And so on

What makes this method work is writing everything and crossing out the completed tasks. This is why we list even the smallest of tasks. Every time you complete a task and go through the act of crossing it off, your brain releases dopamine into your brain because you've achieved something, and it feels good. Your brain wants more of that. When I started out, I even had items like *go to the toilet* and *have a glass of water*, just because it kept me rolling on through my day. There is no task too small or unimportant for your list.

Try it out for yourself and see how beneficial this method can be.

As I said before, you could write an entire book on how to be focused and beat procrastination, and there's a lot out there to choose from. I highly recommend looking into procrastination, or a lack of focus, to see if it is a real problem that's holding you back. However, just following these quick tips can help you make changes. With your mind focused and getting things done, you minimize the stress you're experiencing and ultimately reduce your risk of becoming consumed by overthinking.

Method 7

How to Deal with Stressful External Factors

To conclude our first chapter on overcoming stress that causes you to overthink, let's discuss what is perhaps the most crucial topic of conversation: dealing with stressful situations. While many of us try to be happy and peaceful throughout our lives, we are undoubtedly going to come across stressful situations. They are inevitable.

Whether that's getting road rage at someone cutting you off, breaking down when you need to get to work, receiving a fine or unexpected bill, finding out you've been cheated on, crossing paths with someone who's having a bad day, or even just waking up on the wrong side of your bed, stressful situations are everywhere, coming at you when you least expect it. You need to know how to deal with these situations, so they don't consume you.

If you take stressful situations personally and let them get to you, you're going to feel stressed, anxious, and overthink. I used to handle situations so badly, and I would think, *Why do these things always happen to me? What have I done to deserve this?* and *Why does this always happen to me?* When you start judging yourself for how you handled a situation or what you could have done differently, the risk of overthinking becomes higher.

So, how do you deal with stressful situations?

The most important thing to remember is not to get caught up in any situation. If you can do this, you'll be able to handle anything. Regardless of whether a situation is positive or negative, it's so easy to get lost in the moment, getting caught up in emotions or thoughts. Let's say you're in a situation where your boss is shouting at you and your team because a deadline has been missed. It's so easy to fall into the trap of taking everything personally and as a personal attack—but it's not. Your boss is just projecting how they're feeling, so there's no reason to be scared, upset, or stressed out. Your boss shouting will not make the deadline unmissed and isn't going to make anything better in the long term. Having this mindset is the essence of not getting caught up in the situation and letting it affect you.

Because you're experiencing a situation from a first-person perspective (your perspective), it's very real because it's happening to you, but try to look at each stressful situation from a bird's eye view. In this example, your boss has probably had their boss come down on them extremely hard because the deadline was missed. Because they feel stressed, angry, and upset, they have projected that onto you. It's a chain of events, a sign of a lack of emotional intelligence, especially since your boss is just raging at you because they feel angry.

Because you understand your boss is stressed out and projecting, you know to let them get it out of their system, and they'll be fine once they've cooled off in a couple of hours. Instead of being stressed about the situation, you've remained grounded and focused, allowing yourself to stay peaceful and calm. Basically, you're able to carry on with your day in the best possible way.

Of course, this isn't to say you can't feel emotional. This is inevitable. If something bad happens to you, you're going to feel sad or angry. The trick is to notice the emotions you're feeling and accept them, rather than trying to fight them or acting through them without thought, as your boss did in the example. Far too many people these days live their lives lost in their emotions and acting through them. You've definitely done this, or know people who do. It's very prevalent in children (all children do it) because they're too young to have developed emotional intelligence as it develops during the teenage years.

This is why children cry one minute and can instantly switch to laughing and giggling the next. They are literally just acting through their emotions based on what is happening to them at that moment. They have no consciousness of long-term effects or conscious thinking. They feel something, and it takes them over. Of course, this isn't to say that emotions are unnecessary. All your emotions are valid, but do so consciously, enabling you to understand them and how you think truly and feel about things that happen in your life. It's a great way to get to know yourself.

This is the most important and most effective way of dealing with any stressful situation, and what's great is that it can be applied anywhere, at any time. For example, let's say you've just found out you've been cheated on, and you and your partner are sitting down to talk about it. Yes, you're going to feel angry, and you're going to feel sad and hurt. You're going to feel different emotions, and it's going to be hard to keep your composure and figure out what you're going to do next. Where is the relationship going to go next? What is your next step?

These are big, stressful questions, and it can be so easy to lose control and be abusive, shouting at your partner about how much you hate them and how dishonest they've been, and how much they've hurt you. You may want to express that, but it's probably not going to help long term. Instead, take a moment to be aware of your emotions. Express your needs. Do you need time to process and think? Are you able to forgive? Should your partner leave you alone? It's taking the time to think, feel, and process that will help you remain grounded. At the very least, it's going to stop you from doing or saying something you will regret.

Having the skills to stay focused while acknowledging your emotions and feelings, rather than mindlessly acting through them, will take practice, and you're not going to be perfect. In fact, I believe it's a lifelong process. You will continue to grow into it as you come across more experiences with various impacts and degrees of magnitude in your life. While focusing on this, however, there are other important tips to remember when dealing with stressful situations:

- Do things that make you happy and have breaks from mundane life

- Go into every situation with a positive attitude, or at least have positive intentions

- Have compassion for other people and try to see their side of the story

- Reflect after every stressful situation and consider what you would do next time

- Set limits on how much exposure you have to stressful things and people

- If you need to talk about a stressful situation, don't be afraid to reach out to others

- Write down how you're feeling to vent any negative emotions you may have

We've come to the end of our first chapter. Phew, that was a big one. Hopefully, you've learned plenty of strategies for dealing with stressful situations or are at least thinking about how these points can be implemented into certain areas of your own life. With any luck, you'll be paying much more attention to how you engage with your experiences and how stress affects you.

By being active in your efforts to minimize your stress, you'll actively reduce your chances of overthinking since you'll be more in control and connected with how you think, feel, and live. Don't forget, you can return to this chapter at any time if you need a refresher or a pick me up. It may take a bit of time to break the habits of stressful overthinking, and just reading this book means you've already taken your first step in the right direction towards a happier, healthier future.

Chapter Three

Methods for Managing Anxiety

Tying in with the previous chapter, anxiety is typically a part of most people's lives. This can seem strange to a lot of people. Why are there so many people suffering from anxiety and why is there so much talk about it? With statistics detailing that around 40 million people aged 18 or above in the US alone suffer from some degree of anxiety, and only 36.9% of them receiving treatment for it, it's no wonder it's such a big issue.

If you're an overthinker, you've most likely experienced an anxious mind. Whether you're thinking about old conversations while wishing you did or said something differently, or you're panicking over some upcoming event, situation, or conversation, anticipating all the possible scenarios that could unfold, living with an anxious mind is never easy.

Fortunately, it's something that can be remedied. Just like with stress, if you know the strategies that detail how to deal, cope with, address, and reduce your anxiety, you can reduce its impact on your life because you are actively rewiring your mind for a peaceful, less overthinking life. Fortunately, there are several methods you can teach yourself that can help you soothe your anxious mind and frantic thoughts, both in the moment and over the course of many weeks, months, and years. Let's get into it.

Method 8

Muscle Relaxation Techniques

To begin with, let's aim to ground your anxious mind at the moment when you really feel it coming in. I've always found this extremely difficult because anxiety can start as a slight, underlying feeling that you barely pay attention to. You may feel a pang every now and then, but for me, it crept up over the course of days or even weeks, but it certainly reached a point where it took over and became all-consuming.

Dealing with anxiety at any stage of that process was hard, especially when I didn't believe that anything was wrong. However, when you start paying attention and notice the signs of anxiety creeping in, which is something that only comes with experience, you can do something about it, and you don't have to live with the effects and dread that comes with it.

One of the most proven and effective ways of dealing with anxiety is using a combination of muscle relaxation techniques and deep breathing. These are very similar to the deep breathing exercises we explored in the previous chapter. You are more than welcome to use those breathing exercises for the same results. However, using additional muscle relaxation techniques can provide a fantastic array of benefits when relieving anxiety, the most effective of which is known as Progressive Muscle Relaxation (PMR).

Progressive Muscle Relaxation

PMR is a practice that has been used for a long time. It was first introduced in the 1920s by American physician Edmund Jacobson. Ever since its development, it's been used as one of the most powerful ways to relieve symptoms of stress, anxiety, and chronic pain. Such a powerful technique may sound complicated, but it's straightforward, and once you've mastered the basics, it can become an invaluable life skill.

PMR is the process of tensing and relaxing the muscles around your body with purpose and intention. You need to set aside around ten to twenty minutes to complete one session, meaning that it can be easily incorporated into your daily routine and used whenever it's needed.

Before we jump into the strategy itself, please note that it's recommended you focus on one muscle group at a time for the best results. For example, start with your feet and legs, and end with your face. Don't try to do everything in one go. You may practice sitting or lying down, whichever feels most comfortable for you, and try to make sure you're creating a space where you can do this with ease. This means finding a quiet space with no distractions and a minimal chance of being disturbed, as these can just make you feel worse and more anxious.

Let's get in the process.

While sitting or lying down, inhale slowly and with purpose, and as you do, contract and tense up one muscle group, let's say your toes and your legs or your upper thighs. Tense those muscles while focusing on the feeling for about five to ten seconds and then release. That's it.

Now sit or lay and feel the released muscles for around ten to twenty seconds and then move up or down onto another body part or muscle group and do the same again. When you're releasing your muscles, try to picture, feel, or visualize your muscles actively changing or relaxing. This is a very powerful addition to your practice that will increase the benefits tenfold. Once you've finished every part of your body, the practice is done.

Now, this may sound simple. Surely something so simple could not be as impactful at relieving something as strong and as consuming as anxiety and stress, but the studies, professional opinions, and research show that it does, in fact, work, especially when practiced regularly over long periods of time. The more you practice something, the better at it you'll become, which means you'll enjoy even more benefits.

That's pretty much all there is to it when it comes to PMR. Just keep practicing, or at least try it out several times to see whether it works for you. If it works, then that's amazing. You've just got yourself a tool that can provide endless benefits. If it doesn't, know that you're one step closer to finding out the strategies and techniques that work for you.

METHOD 9

How to Deal with Negative Thinking in the Moment

Taking a little break, I want to explore the concept of negative thinking, defining what it is, what it does to you, and how you can deal with it. Negative thinking and negative overthinking are a massive part of anxiety. Whenever I feel a panic attack coming on, or I'm feeling anxious about something, negative thinking is always there, whether that's thinking I'm going to die or complicating a situation.

Of course, when you talk to anyone about this, they'll suggest a practice like meditation. It's true - mediation is a very powerful and effective tool when it comes to connecting with and understanding yourself. Meditation will help you to notice and acknowledge when you're having negative thoughts instead of being lost and consumed by them and will help you stay grounded and focused.

This is what many meditation guides and gurus will tell you. Imagine you think you're going to lose your job. The company is making cuts, everyone is talking about it, and the boss doesn't seem happy with you. You're convinced that you're going to lose your job, and you become your thoughts. You're not focusing on what you're doing at all. You're distracted at work, when you're with family, and other people in your life, and only thinking about your potential future. This is what gurus refer to as *being your thoughts*.

Meditation is a way to break this habit and instead see your thoughts from an outside perspective. It's as though you're watching your thoughts rather than *being them*. This allows you to look in from a grounded, non-judgmental perspective, therefore staying rational. However, any book, video, or blog post on anxiety and stress will tell you more about meditation, so there's more than enough information for you to explore. If you're looking for a starting point, I highly recommend *The Power of Now* by Eckhart Tolle and getting an app like Headspace, Waking Up, or Insight Timer to help you develop a meditation habit. The trick to meditation is to do it regularly and consistently.

What else can you do to tackle negative thinking, especially when you're in the moment? Sometimes, it's just not possible to sit down and focus on your breathing as required during mediation, especially when you're freaking out and need a fast fix.

Take a Moment to Pause

The second you noticed that you're stuck in a negative thinking pattern, it's essential to take a moment to pause and think. I know, more thinking doesn't sound great, but here we're not thinking about anything particular. We're just taking a moment to become aware of your thoughts and to acknowledge that you're in the thinking loop.

This might sound like meditation, and it is indeed a form of mindfulness, but it's essential for helping your overthinking tendencies to stop. Imagine you're freaking out and getting anxious, worried, or stressed. When your mind is thinking a million thoughts a minute, any decision you make is likely to be irrational and will end up with you digging a deeper hole.

It's time to get into the habit of stopping whatever it is you're doing and taking time out. This can be difficult at first because it's not something you're used to, but with practice over the course of weeks, months, and even years, it becomes an invaluable skill. If you need to remove yourself from a situation, do so. Figure out what you need to do to get yourself out of situations that are causing you to overthink.

Sometimes, all it takes is a single moment or a deep breath to interrupt the constant thinking and to bring yourself back to a grounded state of mind. Get into the habit of doing it, even if you're taking a breath when you're not feeling stressed, just to build that habit, and you'll be able to do it whenever you need to.

Fact vs. Fiction

When negative thinking strikes, there's a high chance that what's going on in your head is very different from your reality. Note that I'm not saying that what you're thinking is invalid or made-up, nor that negative thinking is inherently bad. However, it's when this kind of thinking is overly negative or involves fabricating stories that it becomes a problem.

I had a friend who was terrible at doing this. When we were teenagers, she got upset at teen dramas, relationship issues, and so on, like teenagers do, but she would constantly worry about what people thought about her, what people were saying, and how people were feeling about what was happening. All perfectly valid things to worry about, except that she would worry and think about it so much that she would believe people were talking about her when they weren't. I've seen many examples of this kind of thinking throughout my life, and of course, sometimes I am guilty of it .

When you're stuck in negative thinking patterns, it's essential to take a moment to think about whether what you're thinking about is fact or fiction. If you're telling yourself stories of what's happening, but you don't know the facts of a situation, label that thought pattern as a story and try to focus on the facts, or at least figuring them out.

Understanding Your Thoughts Through Writing

Overthinking may be a bane of your existence because

you're constantly going over whatever it is you're thinking about. However, getting these thoughts out of your head is a great way to understand where they're coming from, what they are, and whether they're actually serving you. That's an excellent point to remember. If a thought isn't serving you well, you don't want to let it influence you and your decisions.

The best way to do this is by getting your thoughts on paper in the form of a thought diary. You can do this in a journal by writing notes in your phone or venting on a scrap of paper you find lying around, although it's highly recommended that you use a dedicated space.

The idea is to write how you're feeling and what you're thinking in the moment that you're thinking it, getting it down in its purest form, and then reflecting on it over time and taking notes to see if there are any patterns in the way you're thinking. You may notice that certain people, situations, experiences, or even places trigger your negative thoughts. If you can identify them, then you'll be able to do something to fix it, rather than mindlessly remaining stuck in your habitual ways of thinking.

A Little Chapter Summary

It doesn't really matter how you go about dealing with your negative thoughts, but the trick is to stop the thinking and to become aware of it. That's the short-term, instant solution, and it all comes through habits. This is why it's important to think about how you think, even when you're not feeling stressed out or anxious. Develop a habit during the good times to make the most of it during the bad times when you really need it.

However, the long-term solutions come from looking back and reflecting on your patterns when you're not in the same anxious state of mind, meaning that you can find rhyme and reason in it, allowing you to do something about it. That's the two-part solution. If you're just starting out on your self-improvement journey, I highly recommend focusing on the first part and getting a level of acknowledgment and acceptance in check for yourself.

Method 10

How to Stop a Panic Attack

If you've suffered from and lived with anxiety for a long time, you've likely experienced a panic attack, and you know how brutal it can be, especially with overthinking. The mind races, your body reacts in such a powerful and intense way, and it is all-consuming. This chapter is about how to deal with and overcome these situations.

Now, it's worth reiterating that everyone is different, and everyone experiences panic attacks in different ways. This means that a solution that works for someone else might not work for you. Of course, it's not a pleasant experience to have a panic attack, flick through this book or the internet to find a solution, which doesn't work. However, going through this process is just that—a process. There are going to be ups and downs. I'm not trying to sugarcoat this journey because it is hard, and there are obstacles you'll need to overcome.

However, with the right information and a willingness to find what works for you, you can find your way forward to a happier, healthier you. Let's take a look at some of the solutions.

The Quick and Easy Methods

You can use some of the methods we've already discussed in this book to overcome panic attacks. Strategies like deep breathing, PMR, and meditating are great ways to overcome a panic attack as it's starting or in full swing. Try them out and see if they work for you.

Recognize the Signs

We all have signs that a panic attack is on its way - I used to feel sick and shaky. I'd start having these feelings of nausea and light-headedness, as though I was going to pass out or felt overly hot but without the temperature symptoms. My legs would go weak, I'd need to sit down, and I wouldn't want to talk to anyone or interact. I'd also feel an overwhelming urge to use the toilet but never actually had to go.

When I first started experiencing panic attacks that were linked to my social anxiety, I would feel these symptoms as they came on but would never peg them as signs of a panic attack. I would simply think I was unwell, that something was wrong, or that I was dying. Of course, this only further perpetuated the panic attacks, and they became more intense. Sometimes these symptoms would take minutes to come on, or they would drag on for hours, building up until it fully hit me.

As I became more experienced with my panic attacks, I started to recognize the signs that one was coming on, and this simple act of recognition helped me tremendously. By thinking, *okay, I'm having a panic attack, not a heart attack, and everything's going to be okay... I just need to let it pass...* I became a lot calmer and would end up just lying on the floor doing breathing exercises until it passed.

Find and recognize your signs in the same way that I did, and you'll take a lot of the panic out of your panic attack.

Focus on an Object

When your panic attack hits and your mind begins to take off, you start to become ungrounded and irrational. It's when the panic starts to kick in, and it will only escalate. More bad feelings make more bad feelings. However, you need to find a way to ground yourself and pull yourself back to reality, and a straightforward way to do this is by focusing on a stationary object.

This can really be anything around you, whether you're holding it in your hands or focusing on it from a distance. Try to direct as much of your attention to that object to stay grounded, stop disconnecting from the present moment, and get out of your head. You can also do this with physical feelings and senses.

My personal favorite is to lie on the ground because it's stable and solid (rather than a soft bed) and feeling the weight of my body pushing into the ground. You can do this now. If you're sitting in bed or in a chair, pay attention to the feeling of your body being in contact with your seat or bed. Can you feel that weighted sensation? Focus on that feeling, and you should notice that your attention is being drawn out of your head and these feelings. If you can practice this while having a panic attack, you'll find it much easier to overcome it without being drawn into it too intensely.

Change Your Environment

Sometimes, it can help to get a fresh perspective when trying to get out of your head, and by this, I mean going for a walk, changing rooms, or stepping outside the room. However, I highly recommend going for a walk because not only do you get the benefits of not being trapped in whatever space you're in, but you also benefit from the light exercise, sunshine, and fresh air.

If you're hyperventilating or unable to move physically, this is not applicable. Instead, focus on an object or close your eyes and focus on the feelings of your body on the ground. However, if you're noticing the signs of a panic attack coming in, heading out for a walk and refreshing your mind could be what you need. It's a simple yet effective strategy.

These are just some of the ways you can stop a panic attack, and chances are you'll need to use a combination of these techniques at different times to manage your panic attacks properly and to overcome them. Just be patient with yourself and forgive yourself when they happen.

Use the following paragraph as a mantra that you can repeat.

Everything is temporary. The feelings I'm feeling right now are temporary. They have come and gone in the past, and the same will happen this time. I won't feel this way forever. I will find peace once more.

Method 11

Reaching Out to Friends, Family, and Getting Support

This method is a tricky one but nonetheless essential. I want to start by saying that you don't have to suffer alone in your personal struggles. Think about the people you love most in your life, such as your friends, family, or coworkers. If they came to you and asked you for help because they were struggling with overthinking, anxiety, or stress, I'm sure you would do what you could to help them. Of course, you would. Although it can be hard to come to terms with, people will do the same for you.

Remember my friend who had the car accident? He experienced suicidal thoughts for months, and it wasn't until he reached out and started to speak about what he was going through and how he felt that he started to overcome it. When you feel like you're fighting your mind, you're unable to figure out yourself since you're fighting against yourself. This is such a simple concept to read about, and it's enlightening to realize that the part of you that's the problem, for lack of a better phrase, won't be able to help itself, for it is itself the issue.

For example, a broken wrench can't fix itself, even though it used to fix other things.

Being able to muster up the courage to openly talk about your mental health issues or something you're going through is a big step. There's the apparent fear of judgment, perhaps that your loved ones would think that you're broken or weak and they won't want you in their life anymore. There's the fear of rejection, opening up to someone, and they just turn you away, unwilling to help you. It's a fear like this that can be absolutely crushing to your confidence, and one you'll believe will make things so much worse for you, but one that can really help you in the long-term.

This part of the chapter covers building up the confidence and courage to ask for help and to take that first step in getting the support you need on your journey to self-improvement and a happier life.

Pick the Right People

This is the most crucial consideration you need to make. You cannot randomly go up to someone you know and just spill everything to them. You're going to get problems. Just because you think someone might help you doesn't mean they will. Maybe they have other things going on in their life and don't have it in them to offer the support you need without sabotaging themselves. Support needs to come from people who can offer it.

So, take a moment to think about someone in your life who is in a place where they can offer support. Granted, you don't always know what's happening, which is why you need to effectively *shortlist* people you want to approach and ask them for help.

Think about the people in your life who you know will offer you support, and you can trust to be open with you and won't judge you. There's no point in asking someone for help if you can't trust them and you can't openly express yourself. If you find yourself hiding facts and not being 100% honest, you're not going to get the help you need.

However, even if the person doesn't understand what you're going through, talking to them can still be helpful if you trust them, and they can support you by listening. Regarding my own mental health issues, I spoke to my father about them. My father is very old fashioned and traditional and would be the first to admit that he doesn't understand mental health issues or why so many people have so many mental health problems, but that didn't stop him from listening and being supportive, making him the perfect person in my life to reach out to.

Share the Story

Once you've decided who to ask for help, open up about what's going on. Start by sitting them down and talking about what's happening. Talk about your experiences and what you've been through. The act of opening up about what you've been through and how you've been feeling is therapy because, much like writing, it is a great way to organize your thoughts and to get them out of your head in a methodical way.

Even if the story is unpleasant and there are some difficult bits you might not want to go into, the idea is to explore it and get it out. Once you've overcome this barrier, you'll be able to explore how it made you feel, how it's affecting you, and what you're going to do about it.

Don't Look for Solutions, Look for Lessons

While seeking help from others is essential, it's important to remember that you're not actually going to them with the hopes of getting them to fix your problems. That's not how this works. If you're dealing with a problem, nobody can say, *oh, do this, and everything will be fixed*. Sure, that could work, but you'll likely find yourself back in the same position.

Instead of looking for solutions to individual problems, be more proactive in learning lessons from both your own experiences and the experiences of others. Once you've learned a lesson, you'll be able to apply what you've learned to either prevent a problem from happening again or at least understand how to deal with it, rather than getting stuck in the issue that you're in now, which leads to overthinking.

Don't Forget Boundaries

You need to have boundaries with the people you speak to, whether that means enforcing them with other people or respecting the boundaries that someone gives you. I know so many friendships and relationships where someone has asked for help, and for whatever reason, a boundary has been crossed, and while everyone has tried to be as helpful and as supportive as possible, it's gone too far.

The relationship lacks boundaries where someone is either too involved, there's no time apart for thinking or reflecting, or the person who wants help is too demanding, and the person giving support hasn't said stop or slow down. While this usually happens out of love, it can destroy relationships. It may be inevitable in some cases, but if you want to keep a relationship going and growing, you have to respect and have compassion for each other's boundaries.

Be clear with each other, communicate how you feel, and listen to the other person. If someone is supporting and helping you make sure you're making time to talk about them and how they're feeling so you know that balance is being achieved. If someone takes some time out for themselves, you need to respect that.

If you can remember this, then you should be able to have a positive relationship when it comes to asking for help and support from other people in your life. Yes, there is a huge step you need to take when it comes to asking for help from others, and it takes a huge degree of confidence to step forward and accept what's happening, but if you're able to do it, you can positively change your life forever.

METHOD 12

Lifestyle Tips to Help You Overcome Anxiety

To conclude this chapter, we're going to dive into one final concept - being proactive in your life and making lifestyle choices that minimize your exposure to anxiety and similar health conditions. You'll see what I mean as we start going through the strategies.

Exercise

You've already heard about all the benefits that exercise can bring into your life, so I won't repeat it. When it comes to treating anxiety, doing regular physical exercise each and every day can do wonders at keeping your symptoms under control.

Simply put, your body was made to move. Ongoing studies show that exercise can improve your mood, reduces inflammation, body tension, anxiety, reduces stress, improves blood circulation, boosts your energy levels, improves your ability to focus, and so much more.

Basically, developing and introducing a simple exercise routine into your life can change your life.

This doesn't mean that you need to join a gym and start bulking up while downing protein shakes. Even if your exercise routine is only a 15-minute walk around your local neighborhood, this seemingly small and simple action can do wonders for your mental health.

Correcting Your Diet

Your diet has such a significant impact on your life, for all the same reasons I spoke about above. If you eat a ton of junk food and stuff that has no nutrients, you're going to suffer and feel bad, which is only going to trigger your anxiety and stress-related feelings.

For example, drinking lots of coffee, caffeine products like energy drinks, or alcohol can induce anxiety-like feelings, and if they start, it's only going to snowball.

Set a Sleep Schedule

Sleeping is vital, yet so many of us don't have a proper schedule, and so many of us live sleep-deprived lives. This is evident from endless studies, such as that 35.2% of US adults sleep less than the recommended seven hours of sleep per night and over 50% of Americans say they feel tired all the time. The impact of this is also incredibly clear.

Around $411 billion is lost every year in the economy due to lack of sleep, and nurses who work 12.5-hour shifts are estimated to make three times more medical mistakes than nurses who work 8.5-hour shifts. In the US, there are over 6,000 annual car wrecks caused by sleepy drivers. Regarding your own health and wellbeing, if you don't get enough sleep, simply put, you're going to suffer for it.

A great way to ensure you're getting a proper, revitalizing amount of sleep is by following the basic sleep guidelines and advice. There are many ways detailing how to get the best sleep, but here are some hard and fast rules everyone should know. They are as follows:

- Get more sunlight during the day
- Reduce your exposure to blue light in the form of screens
- Don't drink caffeinated products late in the day
- Try to avoid naps where you can
- Be proactive with regular exercise
- Try to sleep and wake up at the same time every day
- Take melatonin supplements
- Set up your bedroom for sleep (right temperature, blackout curtains, etc.)
- Get a comfortable bed

These seem obvious, but you'd be surprised by how many people have a broken bed or an old mattress, and how much of an effect this can have on their ability to sleep, and all the negative consequences that come from that.

Start Accepting Your Anxiety

We've touched on this a little already, but one of the biggest steps you'll take in your life is accepting you have anxiety and that it's causing you problems. This admission means you embrace the fact that something is up, but many people believe that ignorance is bliss. If there's nothing inherently wrong, then everything must be okay. But, of course, we know that's not the case, and suppressing your problems will only make them amplify later on.

However, this doesn't mean that you need to identify with your anxiety, or that all hope is lost or there's something wrong with you. Noticing that you have overthinking tendencies (which you have already since you've picked up this book) is a fantastic step because you can start to realize what other areas of your life may be affected, and then you can do something about it, or at least be more proactive in managing the symptoms. We've touched on some ways to implement this step into your life, including:

- Talking to a friend or trusted person about how you're feeling
- Researching your own circumstances online
- Allow yourself to cry
- Find laughter or positivity in any situation
- Journal or start blogging

- Seek out other people who feel the same as you

Dealing with anxiety is a process. It's not something you can snap your fingers and change overnight, and depending on your situation, it may not be something that ever truly goes away. However, don't be disheartened. In fact, there's an opportunity here to feel hope because you know there are endless ways to help yourself and even to help others. It's about going through the process in your journey and figuring out what works for you.

Just remember, you can do it.

Chapter Four

Methods for Calming an Overthinking Mind

We've already covered both stress and anxiety, detailing how they affect your life and how you can deal with it and perhaps even overcome them completely. However, while these are both the causes and effects of overthinking, all of which are intertwined, it's time to tackle the issues of overthinking head-on.

Throughout this chapter, we're going to be looking into six forms of deep-diving, including how to think clearly and with purpose, how to overcome a mind that's plagued with worries and fears, and focusing on techniques and strategies to help you free yourself from all-consuming thoughts. I'll try to keep every part of this chapter as actionable as possible, but remember, knowledge is power, and the more you know, the more tools you'll have in your toolbox to address problems in your life.

Let's get started with a classic.

METHOD 13

Developing the Habit of Meditation

We've spoken about this already, but meditation is an incredibly powerful tool to have when countering all kinds of mental health issues you may be facing in your life. Whether you're dealing with a stressful situation, an intense person, a problem, or you're trying to deal with your anxiety and overthinking, meditation is very beneficial.

However, there are a few widespread misconceptions that we need to address. First, meditation is not the cure. If you're having a panic attack or feeling anxious, you can't just meditate and expect everything to feel better. It's not a solution in this way. Instead, meditation is a practice where you learn how to monitor and become aware of your thoughts, feelings, and emotions. This is why the practice is often referred to as *mindfulness*. It's the process of becoming mindful and conscious of your mind and thoughts, rather than letting your mind run on autopilot and unconsciously.

It's the skill of being aware of your thoughts that can only be achieved through the act of meditation that will help, not so much the act of meditation itself. For years, I believed that people who got stressed would find a quiet place to sit down and relax, close their eyes, and all their problems would go away. That's not how it works. Just like everything else in life, it's a skill that needs to be practiced to work.

Additionally, meditation is not used to *clear the mind*. There are very few people who can close their eyes and make all their thoughts go away. It doesn't work like that. Your brain is always thinking of something. That's its job, and there would be something wrong with it if it wasn't. However, you are not your mind, nor your thoughts, and the act of meditation is all about finding that out.

Take a moment right now to try meditation.

As mentioned earlier, sit down and feel the weight of your body traveling down towards the ground, and feel that sense of contact with whatever surface you're on, be it the ground, bed, or chair. Adjust your body to become comfortable in this position, and once you reach a stable position, try to stay still. Keep focusing on that point of contact and that weighted feeling.

Now, take a moment to watch your thoughts. If you've never meditated before, this can feel weird to sense this feeling that you can watch your thoughts. That's how so many gurus will describe it. You become the watcher of your own mind. Just like you're feeling the grounded sensation, but you're not the sensation itself, aim to do the same with your thoughts.

There are many ways you can go about it. Some people advise that you zero in on your thoughts and focus if you're trying to figure them out, and others prefer to let them come and go without paying much attention to them. When you're starting out, just try to become aware of the thoughts. Close your eyes, take a deep breath, and focus on that weighted sensation.

When you notice yourself getting lost in thought and no longer focusing on the weighted sensations, say to yourself, *"oh, I was lost in my thoughts. That's okay,"* and go back to focusing on the weighted sensation. Again, once your mind goes back to thinking, notice it and pull yourself back to focus on the feeling.

At first, you may find that there are extended periods where you're lost in thought, sometimes for several minutes before you even realize you're not focusing on the weighted feeling. When I started my own meditation practice, I would sit down and try this exact practice with a ten-minute timer and would easily spend 90% of this time in my head before realizing what was going on.

Becoming mindful in this way is a skill that needs to be learned and practiced. Once you start grasping this skill of noticing your thoughts, it will start to branch out into other aspects of your life. Even when you're not meditating, you'll start noticing your thoughts and what you're thinking, becoming conscious of your thinking instead of thinking mindlessly.

This means when you encounter a hard, stressful situation, or you're feeling anxious, or as though you're overthinking, you'll notice your thoughts rather than falling deep into them.

What good is becoming mindful and recognizing your thoughts? After all, you're not stopping them. Well, it's what comes next. You know those times when you have a really messed-up thought, something really dark and horrible, and you think that if anyone knew what you were thinking at that moment, you'd probably get sent away somewhere, and thank god you don't think like that all the time?

Don't worry… everyone has these thoughts from time to time, and it's because they can be so extreme that they stand out, and you become aware of them. The thought itself is so abnormal that it stops you in your tracks, forcing you to become mindful of it. So, what do you do next? Well, you notice the thought and label it as an extreme thought. You don't follow through with it, nor really do anything with it. You just say okay, that's a weird thought, and let it go.

That's exactly what you can do when you're overthinking and having stressful, anxious thoughts. You notice them and say, hey, that's a thought from overthinking, and let it go. Letting go will help you remain grounded and focused in the moment, rather than being carried away by thoughts and feelings. It's all in the mindfulness of the process.

If you're looking to get started, refer to the resources listed in Method 9, including the apps and websites, as these can be great guides to help you find your feet.

Method 14

Being Able to Consciously Think

Whether you're adding to your meditation practice or you find that meditation is for you, this method is about becoming able to think consciously from moment to moment. Much in the same way meditation works, you can become mindful of your thoughts and just do it through other means. While I would advocate for the regular practice of meditation as being the best way to think consciously, let's focus on some other ways you can introduce it into your life.

Of course, practicing these techniques with your meditation practice is going to help you reap more benefits. Let's get into it.

Consciously Complete Chores

A great way to bring conscious thinking into your life is to pay attention to how you feel when vacuuming or doing the dishes or any chores around the house. Since these are tasks you perform daily, they become habitual routines, which are breeding grounds for unconscious thinking. You go through the motions of the task rather than focusing on what you're doing.

So, change this up by bringing focus to the task and thinking about what you're doing and how you feel. Ask yourself, do you feel exhausted, drained, uninspired, or uninterested?

Putting your awareness into the process is what conscious thought entails. It's what it means—bringing focus to what you're doing. You'll discover that accomplishing your regular activities can be enjoyable, especially since you're focused, which reduces the risks that you can fall into old overthinking habits. You may still despise doing chores, but fortunately, you become aware of your thoughts at a time when most people's brains are on autopilot.

You will feel more present in life rather than merely being a mute observer if you give life to your chores and put meaning back into your regular tasks.

Mindful Technology Usage

Let's be real; so many of us have an unconscious relationship with technology. Even as I wrote this sentence, I reached over and grabbed my phone, opened Instagram, scrolled down two or three pictures, then realized that I had just done it without thinking.

When you get on your phone or computer, how do you spend most of your time? Is it scrolling through Facebook and Instagram for hours, checking emails constantly, watching YouTube, or shopping for new gadgets or clothes? So many people waste hours on social media and other unproductive websites every day without realizing it.

Practice mindfulness with your technology and you'll see big improvements in all other areas of your life. You can do this by limiting how much time you spend on your devices, setting limits, deleting apps you don't want to waste time on, not going on your phone before bed, installing website blockers for distracting websites, and so on.

Basically, your aim is to take control of your relationship with tech rather than letting it unconsciously take control of you. It's this kind of discipline and mindfulness that will branch out into other areas of your life.

Introduce Mindful Eating

How often do you pay attention to what you're eating? If you're like most people, probably not that much. You're much more likely to spend your time downing your food while reading or watching the news or playing on your phone than focusing on the sensations of eating itself. Many of us don't really enjoying our food as much as we could because of this, leading to unconscious eating habits, such as eating lots of takeout, snacks, and fast food.

Do you eat foods that give you life and nurture your cells, or do you feed your body chemical-laden, processed meals with little to no nutritional value? When you live a fast-paced life, it's all too simple to drive through the nearest fast-food restaurant and pick convenience over nutrition, but you might not even realize how often you do so.

You can choose to eat more whole, fresh fruits and vegetables instead of fast food or frozen dinners. You can change your habits, and what you eat can be either healthy or unhealthy.

Consider what you're about to eat before you swallow it. One of the most fundamental parts of conscious thinking is food. Just like meditation, paying attention to your food allows you to train your focus, which will only help you apply this focus in other areas of your life.

What's more, you're going to start enjoying food a whole lot more!

Get Out of the Comfort Zone

There isn't a better way to put your mind and spirit to the test than to take them into new territory. You excite your soul and invalidate negative thinking habits by attempting something fresh and new. There's no better way to get your mind thinking consciously than to put it in a position where you need to focus on what you're doing and how to move forward.

It's so easy to spend so much of our life in the comfort zone, doing what we know while only branching out here and there into safe territories when it's on our terms. Putting yourself in difficult situations allows you to learn the skills necessary for dealing with stressful situations,. Of course, this takes a bit of confidence and a leap of faith, but you've got it in you; you just need to take that step and enjoy the process. Take your time and let things grow. You can't expect the results straight away.

An example of this could be putting yourself in the deep end and saying you need to give a speech at a special event such as a wedding.

You may be terrified of how others will react, but by embracing your anxieties, you can develop new thinking patterns that promote optimism and confidence rather than despair and anxiety. You can practice positive thinking before you step up on stage.

You may transform the phrases *My speech isn't good enough; everyone will hate it,* and *I'm too nervous to speak on stage* into *I composed this speech from my heart, so it can't be awful,* and *I am fully capable of reading this speech to everyone in this room.*

Keep up practicing these techniques and introducing them into your life where you can, but don't be afraid to get creative. If you want to answer emails, walk around your house, have a shower, or become conscious in any other aspect of your life, do what works for you.

Method 15

How to Use CBT Training

You've probably heard of CBT (Cognitive Behavior Therapy). It's practice has taken center stage in the last few years within the mental health world as one of the most effective treatments for helping people think consciously, overcome overthinking tendencies, and improve overall mental health.

This is a hard practice and might be difficult at first. As we've discussed, all your thoughts are connected in the same way overthinking is linked to stress and anxiety, or can be a standalone concept. CBT is about exploring this connectedness. Once you have some kind of understanding, you'll be able to move forward in your life, free from the obstacles or thought patterns that once held you back.

It takes time to develop the skills, so you need to be patient with yourself and allow yourself time to develop your abilities. In some cases, you're probably going to need professional assistance, whether from a licensed therapist, counselor, or psychologist,.

This is what we'll be focusing on now. These CBT techniques can be practiced at home, and we'll explore them step-by-step. So, let's get into the first part.

Changing Your Perspectives

There's a technique known as Cognitive Restructuring, which is very effective when it comes to changing your perspectives and outlooks on life. This ties into a lot of what we've said already in terms of negative thinking, overthinking, and dealing with depression, anxiety, and other such conditions.

The process is simple. Whenever you next catch yourself feeling depressed, anxious, or locked into a cycle of overthinking, ask yourself this question:

What are you thinking about, doing, or feeling that is making you feel the way you're feeling? Is there anything you're struggling with in your life that is causing you distress?

It may be obvious what you're going through (perhaps a life-changing event is happening), or maybe the answers are less obvious. Perhaps nothing comes to mind right away, or a few things do, but you're not really sure which one it is. The trick here is to write down everything you're thinking about, even if it's just a list.

Look at these aspects of your life, see how they tie together and the links between the thoughts. This way, you will find your triggers, allowing you to start changing your perspective. Whether you want to stop worrying about something so much, or you want to be proactive in making a change in your life, this is a great way to go about it.

This can get long and complicated. For me, during my younger years and as a teenager, I always had a problem with money. I would spend endlessly and never save, constantly ending up having overdrafts. But I didn't know why I did it to myself. I wanted to save and be financially secure, but I would impulsively spend any time I started doing well and put myself back to square one. Why?

Through CBT, I was able to figure out that when I was growing up (which is a time of your life where many of your problems will stem too), my parents were always arguing about money and financial issues, so I grew up seeing money as a problem. In a strange, mostly unconscious way, I didn't want to have money because I saw it as a negative thing in life because of my childhood experiences. When I realized this thought process, I could change my perspective and ultimately change my life!

Finding Balance

Overthinking and other mental health problems are usually caused by an imbalance of thinking, and most likely, the thoughts you're experiencing during the worst times are flawed because of this. You'll be thinking and focusing on just one specific point of conversation or perspective without the ability or insight to look at the bigger picture. This causes the imbalance, and therefore the problems commence, especially when you're making decisions with this state of mind.

For example, if you think that you're nervous talking in front of crowds of people and you say, *I couldn't talk to a large group of people, I would be so nervous*, of course, you're going to think this way. If you're ever in a position where you would need to speak in front of a large group, you're going to feel nervous and panicked.

From then on, every time you're in the same situation, you're just reinforcing that point of view, setting it deeper into your mind. However, stepping back into reality, the truth is that you might not be scared of speaking in front of crowds, you've simply told yourself you are. This is the crux of imbalanced thinking.

Observe how your brain rationalizes decisions made out of fear or avoidance, and ask yourself, *"What evidence do I have for that thought? Is there any objective evidence that things will go wrong, or am I simply guessing?"*

Consider whether any other ideas would be more balanced or beneficial. What new feelings would arise if you adjusted your mental process to be less scared or negative? If you attempt to improve the balance of your ideas, your emotions and behaviors are likely to improve as well.

Learn to Be Kind to Yourself

It's incredibly easy to get caught up in negative self-talk

without realizing it, especially when you're going through the CBT process, and you hit an obstacle, have a hard day or mess up, and you get lost in old cycles when you think you're making progress. However, repeatedly berating yourself will not instill the confidence necessary to help you get better at anything.

Replace negative thoughts with something kinder when you see them creeping in, such as, *"Why can't I just get it together?"* or *"Other people don't have this difficulty"* with thoughts like, *"I'm focusing on it, and so I can do something about it,"* or *"I'm on my journey, and I'm learning how to deal with these things. It just takes time and an open mind, both of which I have."*

This isn't to say that you should make excuses for yourself when you've made a mistake or done something wrong; instead, it's to say that you should give yourself the grace you generally save for only others.

Summarizing CBT

Very basically, this is the process of CBT. To wrap it up, it's the process of realizing your thoughts, giving them replacement thoughts, and then going through this process repeatedly, finding the limiting or oppressive thoughts that are holding you back and then replacing them with new ways of thinking. As the title of this book suggests, you're actively rewiring your mind to stop overthinking and to have a more positive mindset.

If you want to break it down a little further and make it a little more memorable, many people remember the five steps of CBT, which go as follows:

- Find troubling, distressing, or uncomfortable areas of your life

- Become aware of the thoughts, feelings, and emotions tied with those situations

- Find the negative or limiting areas within those thought patterns

- Reshape those thoughts and replace them with more beneficial ones

- Repeat the process throughout your life

I'll say it one more time, but the more you practice something, the better at it you'll become, and it's the same with CBT. It's a continuous process that constantly helps you to evaluate and improve parts of your life, especially in areas where you're overthinking. If you need guidance, there are many resources online, or you could seek help from a professional.

METHOD 16

How to Deal with Fears and Worries

Fear is a limiting belief. So is worry and anxiety. It doesn't matter what you're scared or frightened of, whether it's physical, a situation or experience, person, or anything else, the vast majority of the time, these fears are irrational or become irrational, and end up holding you back.

I once knew a girl in my neighborhood that was bitten by a dog and was terrified of dogs for most of her life. Quite understandably. That's a very traumatic experience. However, just because you were bit by a dog when you were younger, that doesn't mean that every dog you meet will bite you. It's a very isolated incident and very unlikely to happen again.

Therefore, this fear of dogs becomes a limiting belief that could, in many ways, hold you back, such as if a potential partner of yours wanted to get a dog. Whether you're facing a traumatic fear or an everyday fear or phobia, like a fear of spiders, or are worried about something, such as an upcoming tough conversation with a friend, there are fears and worries (both of which lead to overthinking) that can be addressed, acknowledged, and overcome. This chapter discusses a few of the ways you can do just that.

Facing Your Fears

The more you think something, the more you believe it, regardless of whether it's true or not. The same applies to fears and worries. If you don't face your fears, then you're cementing the fact that you're scared of whatever it is you're scared of, ultimately making the fear worse. Yes, it's scary to face your fears, but the more you do it, the faster and easier you'll get over it.

For example, if you're scared of spiders and there is a spider in your house that you don't want to put outside, then you need to at least try to get it outside. Sure, you might not get it the first time, but the more you try eventually, you'll be able to, and sooner rather than later, you'll be able to overcome your fear.

Practice a Relaxation Technique

We've already spoken about muscle relaxing techniques like PMR, meditation, and so on. If you're feeling worried, fearful, or scared, practicing one of these techniques is a great way to ground yourself and to stop the panic. Of course, the technique above about facing your fears is probably not what you want to hear, but it's nonetheless essential if you want to overcome the obstacle.

What you can do is to combine these two techniques and, when you're starting the process of facing your fear, practice a relaxation technique to calm down and get yourself in a grounded state of mind before moving forward.

Let's say you're tackling the spider issue in your home. When you know there's an opportunity to face your fears, the overthinking mind, of course, kicks in and starts doing its thing, which will only make you panic and even more scared. As we've discussed, you can interrupt these thought patterns by acknowledging them and then calming them with a technique that works for you.

When you're in a calm and collected state of mind, you'll be able to face your fear and overcome it in time.

Take Time to Know Yourself

There will be triggers in your life of things that make you scared and worried, and there will be things you can do to make yourself feel better and to ease said fears. However, this is only possible if you proactively take time to get to know yourself and acknowledge how your mind works. This is why so many people recommend writing a journal or keeping a diary since you're creating the time to learn about yourself and a safe space to reflect.

However, if you feel specific fears are really holding you back, you don't need to keep an entire journal. Let's say you have a fear of public speaking, but it's still something you need to do. You can have a slip of paper in your pocket with a simple message to yourself saying that everything is okay and this is something you can do. Just by knowing that it is there, you'll feel calmer and know that you're capable.

Even having a little note saying something seemingly small like *you can do it* can be enough to motivate you to take that step of facing your fears. If you need, have the note written by someone else you trust. It really doesn't matter what the *what* is; what matters is that you're finding the little solutions that help you move forward.

Define Your Purpose

Facing your fears becomes easier when you take the time to identify your purpose for doing something. Public speaking, for example, is not for everyone, and some people will shy away from it their entire lives. However, if you want to succeed in a career that requires public speaking, you need to overcome your fear of public speaking.

Ask yourself what you want more. Do you want to succeed and overcome your fear, or do you want to stay where you are and potentially miss out on the career of a lifetime because you couldn't step up? Putting a spider outside or not getting in an elevator because you're scared may not seem like a big fear you need to overcome. But that couldn't be less true.

Find your meaning in overcoming your fears, making the process so much easier and much more effective. For example, you might not care to overcome your fear of spiders for yourself, but if you have children who are susceptible to copying their parent's actions, do you want your kids to be afraid of them? The reason for addressing this fear would be enabling your children to grow up without this fear.

Finding meaning, positivity, and purpose in your actions can dramatically help to motivate you. With that, we come to the end of this little chapter. In summary, if you're scared of something in your life, the best thing you can do is to lean into it and face it. That's hard, to begin with, but overcoming a fear is something that can help you in your life.

METHOD 17

Seeking Therapy and Professional Services

If you feel like you're living with a fear that's severely holding you back and preventing you from living the life you want, especially if you've tried doing something about it but you seem unable to make significant progress, then it is time to seek professional assistance. This could be in the form of counseling, seeing a therapist, or a psychologist.

Lots of people talk about how hard it is to start therapy, but it's quite simple. You choose a therapist and get in touch with them. You talk about what you want to talk about and discuss whether you're a good fit, and then you start having sessions. Self-help sessions like this can take a bit of time to get off the ground and to start seeing some benefits. You may need to take some of your internal walls down and get stuck into some harder topics before you start and understand yourself and your fears. Once you have understanding, you can start working on them, whether you're rewiring your thinking and thought patterns or actively overcoming the fear directly.

So, getting started is easy, but it's not a fluid process. This chapter is all about sharing some tips I've collected from research, personal experiences, and experiences of others in my life to help make the process as smooth as possible and for you to get the most out of your professional help experience.

Take Time to Find the Right Professional

Not all therapists are equal, and they're human. If you start sessions, take a few sessions to see if you click, but if you're not clicking and you're uncomfortable or feels as though it's not working for you, ask for a referral or look for another professional. Therapists expect this to happen, so don't feel bad. Remember, this is all about making time for yourself and bettering yourself, which means doing things that work for you.

If you're with a therapist and it doesn't work the first time, it doesn't mean that therapy isn't for you and you should give up. Instead, just take your time finding the right professional for you.

Make Sure You're Honest

You're not going to get the most out of professional help if you're not open and honest. Sure, you might want to take your time before opening up to a stranger, but a good therapist will be open and honest with you to help you build a relationship where you can be yourself and talk openly without censoring yourself.

If you're in a session where you find yourself lying or not being completely honest about something, you need to ask yourself why you're doing that. What's holding you back, and what do you need to do to overcome it?

It Takes Time to Work

A common belief many people have about therapy that when you are in a session, you'll tackle a difficult subject that makes you want to break down and cry in front of a stranger. This is entirely possible, but it's important to remember that while therapy can be hard in this way, it is rewarding and takes time to see the results.

There's a chance that things will be hard before they get better, but like everything else we've discussed in this book, being proactive in taking that leap of faith with yourself will bring benefits into your life that can, and almost certainly will, positively change your life forever.

You need to have patience with yourself and the process. It takes time. This could be weeks or months before you feel better, but when you consider that you're probably trying to deal with traumas and problems you've been holding onto for years or decades, it makes sense why it can take so long.

It's Not a Selfish Process

When I had therapy sessions, I repeatedly thought about how selfish it was to go to this person's office and just talk about myself and my own life for an hour a week. The compassionate side of me wanted to talk about my therapist's life and what she was going through. I had an urge to make it balanced.

However, as she kindly reminded me, there was no other time in my life where I had an opportunity to sit and talk to someone in as much detail as we did, especially in a space that promoted trust, openness, and honesty. Taking care of yourself is not selfish. There's no way you'll be able to show up in your other relationships or in any part of your life as the best version of yourself if you don't set aside time to become the best version of yourself.

A Note on Money

Before the end of this section, we need to talk about money because therapy or any kind of professional help can be expensive. It makes sense. Becoming a therapist requires thousands of hours of training and years of education, and if therapists aren't paid to do their jobs, they can't provide the service.

However, there's the drawback that not everybody can afford the service, and if you're in this position, it can be a hard choice to make. Do you want to spend money to help yourself get better but live financially tighter in the meantime, or just carry on as you are? If you're experiencing money problems or have a family to look after, this is not a light decision in any sense of the word.

The best thing to do is to link back to what we've already discussed. You need to proactively find a therapist that suits your needs. Find one you get on with and can be open and honest with, but also make sure the cost falls within your budget. Talk with the therapist to see what they can do for you so you're able to find an agreement that suits you both.

With that, we come to the end of Chapter Four and our journey into overcoming the fears and worries we may be living with. In fact, that takes us to the end of this section dealing with the issues you're living with when it comes to stress, anxiety, and overthinking, and now we're going to switch things up by moving onto how you can move forward from this part of your life. You've set out on your journey to overcome your issues, and now is the time to focus on what new areas you're heading into.

Chapter Five

Methods for Happiness and Rewiring Your Mind

The last part of your journey is about taking steps towards becoming the person you want to be. Leaving behind and growing out of the old, overthinking, anxious, or nervous part of yourself, and taking the unique opportunity to step into becoming whoever you want to be. While this means different things for different people, the main consensus is that people want to be happy, healthier, and more at peace with the things going on in their lives.

This chapter is about providing you with the tools you need to step into this version of yourself. These are tried and tested strategies proven to help improve wellbeing, sense of self, self-esteem, self-confidence, happiness, sense of peace, and so much more. When you're ready to begin this part of your journey, this chapter is here for you.

Method 18

The Art of Helping Others That Ends Up Helping You

While many self-help guides, articles, and books will detail the things you can do to help yourself and get into a better place, the truth is that one of the best ways to help yourself is to help others. By helping others, you're taking responsibility for them and their needs and becoming a valuable person in the process.

Remember the discussion about our ancestors who lived in caves? Quick recap - if you were living on your own and were hurt or became ill, you wouldn't last long in the wild. Instead, working together means people can survive more challenging times and prosper, by splitting work between people or looking after each other. The load is always lighter when shared.

We've come a long way since then and while being alone and working for yourself isn't really a matter of life or death, our instinct to be valuable and to compassionately help others is still very much a part of who we are and ingrained into our genetics. That means helping someone will still bring the same natural rewards it did then. Human beings are basically beings with old, outdated computer software living in a modern world.

Some of the proven and most researched benefits of helping others include:

- It feels good and releases feel-good chemicals
- It brings purpose into your life
- It nurtures a sense of belonging
- It gives you perspective in the lives of others
- You create a butterfly effect where people you help will want to help others
- You reduce feelings of stress and anxiety
- You nurture healthier and more committed relationships between other people
- You develop a more positive thinking mindset

With so many potential benefits, how can you proactively help others? Let's explore.

Volunteering Your Time to Others

The most traditional way to help others is to actively volunteer your time, which starts with looking for opportunities. You could volunteer your time to a charity or a cause. If someone is hosting a party, moving house, or looking for help with their studies, you can offer to help them out. This is all you need to do to get started.

This is commonly referred to as community service, and there are so many opportunities. You just need to look for them. These could include causes like working in an animal shelter, volunteering at a food bank, or just helping a friend move a couch. If you're struggling to find something, try actively reaching out to people and organizations like libraries, colleges, and animal shelters to see what opportunities they have available.

Ask People What They Need

The next step is to create opportunities to help others. Many people don't want to ask for help because they don't want to seem needy or like they're taking advantage of people. Some people don't want to ask for help because they don't want to admit they need it. You can overcome this state of mind when you offer help and ask someone what they need, breaking down that initial barrier of them feeling too uncomfortable to ask.

You don't need to ask if everyone needs help all the time, but keep an eye open for opportunities in disguise. For example, I visited my parent's house, and they had some bricks delivered that they were going to put down around their pond. The pallet was dropped off in the driveway, and when I arrived and found out what they were, I asked if they wanted a hand taking them to the pond area. They accepted, and I helped. That's all there is to it.

After we had dinner, my mother cleared away the plates and started washing them up, so I asked if she wanted help drying them and putting everything away. Little actions like this will create strong and meaningful bonds with people and give you purpose and meaning in your life. With purpose and meaning comes peace and happiness.

You'll also be able to find more opportunities to help people if you listen to people more. Hear what they're saying, aim to be non-judgmental, and give them your full attention. It's through listening that you'll be able to find out what people are struggling with, enabling you to spot opportunities to help.

Sharing is Caring

By far, one of the simplest ways to help people is to share what you have, and this doesn't just mean sharing what you have. It means putting people first in your mind to let them know you're thinking about them and their well-being. For example, seemingly small gestures like holding a door open for someone or offering them a cup of coffee when you make yourself one can brighten their day and make them feel appreciated.

Keep your eyes open for unexpected opportunities to show kindness. This can take a bit of practice, but it's sure to make you develop a kind-hearted, warm, and loving mindset towards other people, and likely to get you out of your own head and thinking about others, hence less overthinking and more happiness!

To summarize, you basically want to go through life training your mind to look for opportunities to help others. Of course, you don't want to do this at your own detriment. If you need to focus on yourself and your own well-being, this needs to be a priority, but it's always a good idea to be thinking about how you can achieve a balance with this kind of thought process.

Method 19

Becoming a Social Butterfly

Don't panic. I'm not asking you to become the most charismatic extroverted person in the world, or to be friends with everyone to achieve happiness. When I say become a social butterfly, I mean approach the art of being social in the same way as a butterfly lives its life. Careful, lightly, and with grace. Let me explain.

Everybody sits somewhere on the scale of being an introvert to an extrovert. If you're introverted, don't force yourself to become the most talkative person you can be because you'll be pretending to be someone you're not and burning yourself out in social situations. Instead, learn who you are and what situations work best for you.

Take a moment to think about it. Are you introverted or extroverted? Do you prefer to be in large groups of people with lots of friends that you dip and dart between, or do you prefer having a small group of friends that are dedicated to each other? Whichever works for you, figure it out and then lean into making those relationships what you want and need them to be.

Being social in the ways that work best for you will bring so many scientifically proven benefits into your life, including:

- Reduced feelings of loneliness, isolation, stress, anxiety, and depression
- Improved condition of mental health
- Reduced blood pressure
- Reduced risk of Alzheimer's, diabetes, and generally improved physical health
- Improves your quality of life
- Promotes a sense of purpose
- Improves your confidence levels and self-esteem

Let's talk about how you can be more connected in your existing relationships.

Work on Being a Better Listener

Developing your listening skills is one of the most important skills you can have as a human being because it allows you to communicate with others properly, gives you insight into what they're saying, and allows you to form connections properly. Many people go through their day-to-day lives without listening properly, instead getting lost in their own overthinking patterns.

When you're conversing with someone, take a moment to figure out whether you're actually listening to them, and try to notice when your thoughts start to drift and you're losing focus. Then take a deep breath and give the other person your full attention. Other proven tips include:

- Face someone and make eye contact with them
- Minimize distractions, like not using your phone when they are speaking
- Keep an open mind and don't judge
- Don't force solutions onto someone, but listen to their issues
- Don't interrupt
- Repeat what someone is saying in your own words to prove you've listened to what they're saying

Ask Questions

One of the best ways you can nurture a strong relationship with someone is to ask them questions about what they're saying. You can use this technique in different ways. For example, if someone is talking about something and you don't really understand what they're saying, you can ask for clarity by having them reword what they're saying. Another example would be if someone is talking about something that's interesting to them that they clearly want to share, but they don't want to keep talking about themselves. Asking a question in this situation shows you're interested in what they have to say and encourages them to keep going.

Make Memories Together

When developing relationships with people, you'll want to make memories that will bring you closer. Positive memories like taking a trip with someone, going to the movies, playing games, or just hanging out and having nice conversations or laughing together are great ways to do this. However, instead of focusing on making these things happen, focus instead on creating the opportunities for this to happen.

This means you need to organize and plan meetups and events for you and your close ones to enjoy. This is where it pays to know yourself. If you're introverted, plan intimate meetups. And if you're extroverted, feel free to do something a little more public.

Be Free from Judgments

It's essential that you approach every interaction with an open mind. We all have preconditioned judgments that cloud our judgment, but these will only keep you disconnect from other people. If someone says something and you already have strong opinions on the topic of conversation or the person, you're going to end up not really listening because you already think you know what they're saying and forcing your own opinions.

Relax and take a step back. Try to approach every situation with an open mind and listen to people. Not only will this help you understand people, but it's also a precious skill that can benefit you in all social situations as you'll be able to deal with anyone.

Connect with the Right People

The final thing to remember - you need to make sure you're investing your time with the right people and not wasting your energy on people that don't serve you. You probably already know I'm talking about toxic people in your life, and there's been a point in everyone's life where we've had toxic people stick around for a little too long.

Bear in mind that this doesn't mean all people are inherently toxic, but maybe they are just going through something and aren't dealing with it in a healthy way, or perhaps you don't have very good boundaries with this person, and it's become an unbalanced relationship that's doing you more harm than good.

It's important to make decisions in your life about where and who you're spending your energy on. If you're giving a lot of attention to someone who isn't balanced, and the relationship doesn't feel right, th you need to explore this and make a decision. I'm not saying you need to cut people out of your life. Of course, that's an option, but it's more important to either distance yourself for a bit, create boundaries, tell the other person how you feel, or work on addressing the issues.

If these attempts are in vain, you may decide to move on and invest your time in other relationships that are more balanced and beneficial.

METHOD 20

Developing Your Positive Self Talk

Since we spoke about addressing and overcoming your negative thinking patterns earlier, it's only fair that we take time to explore how you can promote positive thinking in your life. We've discussed processes like CBT that actively rewire your brain for positive thinking by reducing negative thinking, so this is introduction of other tips and strategies you can use throughout your daily life to maintain a positive and productive mindset.

What is Self-Talk?

Self-talk is the term describing the internal chatter you

have in your mind. This is the voice in your head, your stream of thought and consciousness. If you're able to train this stream of self-talk to be positive, then you'll benefit in so many ways, including:

- Increased confidence

- Higher self-esteem
- Higher motivation
- Higher productivity
- Better relationships

How to Train Your Self-Talk to Become More Positive

The very best way to think positively is to notice your negative thoughts and to mindfully rephrase them. Here are some examples.

- Negative: I can't change my mind because everyone will hate me.
- Positive: I am always in control of my decisions and have the right to change my mind.
- Negative: I was humiliated by my failure.
- Positive: I'm pleased with myself for even attempting this situation in the first place. It was a big step for me to even try.
- Negative: I'm out of shape and overweight. It's probably best if I don't even bother trying to be healthier.
- Positivity: I am capable and strong, and I want to improve my health, even if it takes a long time to do so.

When you start out, focus on recognizing your negative thoughts and then rewording them into more positive language. This may sound like simple, but it can make a significant difference, especially in the long term when the negative thought patterns can become second nature.

In addition to this strategy and the others discussed in this book, it's advisable that you try and surround yourself with positive, like-minded people. If you're surrounded by people who constantly complain and moan, it can be incredibly hard to keep a positive mindset.

Method 21

Setting Goals and Having Aspirations

Life is an interesting journey, with plenty of opportunities and experiences that are random, out of the blue, and completely life changing. However, while excitedly unexpected, having goals and a sense of direction is essential when it comes to being happy and peaceful. According to modern research, having goals and aspirations can be beneficial in several ways, including:

- You know where to spend energy in your life
- Create the chances to feel personal satisfaction when completing goals
- Allows you to focus, maintain productivity, and takes the thinking out of daily life
- Gives you a way to create boundaries and manage your expectations
- Allows you to make clear decisions

Basically, you can wander through life not really knowing what you're doing, or you can give yourself direction and understanding moving forward. Imagine tackling a project at work. If you don't know what you're doing, you're going to waste time trying to figure it out and where to start. This uses so much of your limited brainpower just trying to get started.

Instead, if you break down your project into goals and targets, you know exactly what you're aiming for and what you're supposed to be doing. This means less time spent thinking about what you're doing and more time working. The same applies to your life.

What do you want to do? Do you want to make online content, stream, or YouTube videos? Do you want to write books? Do you want to start a business or focus on your family? Do you want a vacation, to travel the world or a new car? Do you have a dream job?

Whatever it is you want to do, it's always best to get focused and have a concrete goal in your mind. The clearer your goals, the more you know what you're aiming for. This means more direction and more focus on getting stuff done. The more stuff you're getting done, the more satisfied and happier you'll be. Do you really need me to explain this? It's the process of making your dreams come true.

Let's explore how you can set goals that work.

Break It Down

If your goal is big and scary, you're never going to achieve it because it's too broad and unmanageable. You can't just sit down and hope to write a book. You need to take your goal and break it down into manageable and achievable steps. This way, you'll be far more productive and far more motivated because you'll be smashing through small steps.

For example, hosting a dinner party is a big task. However, breaking it down into steps makes it easy.

- Pick a menu
- Decide dress code
- Make a playlist
- Get drinks
- Send invitations
- Think of party games

These are all easy tasks that you can apply your energy to, rather than dealing with the mammoth concept of organizing a good party. By breaking things down step by step and setting yourself manageable goals, you can achieve more and be rewarded for completing what you set out to achieve.

Be Clear with Your Goals

The problem with most people setting goals is that they are too broad with their descriptions, and therefore it makes it far more challenging to follow through. Simply put, if you don't know what your goal is, how are you going to see it through to the end? You may have a rough idea of what it's about, but if you don't have clarity, you'll end up giving up and leaving it by the wayside.

Taking the previous example - writing a book is a big goal, but it's not very clear nor precise. Setting the goal to write one page per day, however, is a very actionable goal that's direct, achievable, and easy to follow through with. The simpler the thinking part of your goal setting, the easier it will be to go through with it.

Create a Measurable Metric

The next step is coming up with a way to measure your success. This is a metric or an action that once achieved, you'll think, *yes, I've done this part of the task,* guaranteeing the release of dopamine and boosting your motivation.

The metric will depend on what you're doing and what you're trying to achieve. If you're writing a book, you may set the goal to write 500 words a day or finish proofreading two pages. If you're working out, you may plan to spend an hour at the gym, run one kilometer in five minutes, or to do a certain number of reps.

This goes hand in hand with making your goals clear and precise. You're taking the thinking out of the process because 99% of the time, it's the overthinking that's holding you back from doing what you want to do. Instead of thinking about what you're writing, how much you're going to do when your breaks are, and so on, you just know that you need to write X words by the end of the day.

That's it. It's clear. It's easy. This approach gives you everything you need to act.

Goals Define Your Actions

Speaking of action, when you're setting goals, you need to make sure you're choosing the correct language to describe the action you're going to take. In the examples we've discussed, you can see the language I've used is very actionable, such as writing a page or doing a specific number of reps.

What's not actionable is setting a goal like *I must work out, I must eat healthily, I should use my phone less,* and so on. Describe the action and then act. *I must work out* becomes *I will do a one-hour run in the gym three times a week. I must eat healthily* becomes *I will count my calories and create weekly meal plans that I'll stick to. I should use my phone less* becomes *I shall put a screen time monitor on my device and only use my phone for two hours, but never an hour before I go to bed.*

I'm repeating this to cement the concept in your mind, which will allow you to apply it in any area of your life, no matter what you're doing. The clearer and concise your goals, the easier it will be to follow through. The more precise you make the descriptive action, the easier your mind will follow through with it.

Make Your Goals Challenging but Attainable

An exciting consideration you need to make is how difficult your goals are. I know what you're thinking. Hold up, you told me to make my goals simple and easy. That's true, the action and the detail of the goal should be simple at its core, but to be satisfying and rewarding, it needs to be somewhat challenging.

For example, a target of 200 words is a manageable goal, but if you could easily write 1,000 words in an hour, a goal of 200 is unsatisfying and not challenging. On the other hand, you don't want to make your goal so challenging that it's impossible, such as writing 2,000 words an hour.

Science has proven that the sweet spot for both motivation and productivity is creating a goal that is manageable but only at a push. You need to find what you can do comfortably and then aim a little further. If you can run 10km per hour, aim to do it in 55 minutes as your challenge. If 55 minutes is challenging, aiming to shave a minute off down to 59 minutes is a challenging yet attainable goal.

This way, pushing yourself outside your comfort zone and achieving what you set out to do will feel a lot more satisfying, which will only motivate you to do more!

Set Yourself Deadlines

The final element of goal setting is, setting realistic deadlines to achieve your goals. This is linked to making your goals attainable but adding enough pressure makes it a challenge. After all, writing 2,000 words of your new novel might be a good goal, but taking a year to do it is not.

Just like the section above, you need realistic goals that are just challenging enough that you're pushed to the edges of your comfort zone as this is where you're going to grow and become a more capable, motivated, productive, and able person.

It might take a little time to experiment with what kind of deadlines work for you. Sometimes they may be too challenging, and sometimes you may slack off, but this is all part of ythe process as you get to know and understand yourself and the way you work.

Summarizing Goal Settings

For now, this should be enough to keep you going with your goal setting, and incorporating what you've learned here should be enough for you to see significant improvements in your ability to get things done. This leads to being happier, greater productivity, and a generally more satisfying life. It doesn't matter what you're doing; these rules can be applied.

If you're looking for more insight into this, look up how to make and follow through with SMART goals, which is the massively popular tried and tested method for setting goals that has helped individuals, organizations, and businesses worldwide.

Method 22

Only Focusing on What You Have Control Over...

This is an interesting topic. This book, and pretty much every other book I've written and plan to write, is based on scientific studies and research, but we can't talk about the ideas of happiness and peace without looking into the more philosophical side of things. Happiness can, to a degree, be rated on a spectrum, and you can measure it, but there are certainly elements that can't be observed.

For example, how do you measure how much stress you're experiencing because a situation you can't control? How do you observe how in control of a situation you are? What percentage of your life are you in control of? These are all hard questions with hard answers, but they're incredibly important to talk about because your perspective directly impacts your happiness.

If you've been involved in a self-help journey, then you've properly heard of the power of letting go of what you can't control because it's only going to make you miserable. While we like to feel in control, the truth is that you only ever have control over one part of your life, and that's control over the decisions and choices you make.

Here's an example of what I'm talking about in the form of a series of events.

- You're in a relationship
- You start working longer hours
- You and your partner start arguing with each other
- Your partner cheats on you one night
- You talk about it with your partner
- You decide to give things another go
- You end up cheating on your partner
- You break up
- You get back together
- You break up again

What stages of this life experience do you have control over, and which areas do you not have control? The truth is, you have control over all and none of it. Yes, that makes things very confusing, but here's the deal—you only ever have control over the decisions you make. If you started working longer hours and your partner hated it because they felt lonely, you don't control your partner's feeling.

They could decide to leave, to stay, to get some hobbies, or to work on their feelings to overcome the negative emotions. You can talk to your partner about what they're going through and offer suggestions, but you can't change how they feel. If they decide to move on or deal with it, that's their choice, regardless of what you say or do.

However, you could choose to walk away. You could choose to get angry when your partner mentions feeling lonely, say you're done, and leave them. That's a choice you could make. This is a concept that affects every single part of your life, and it's making you miserable.

You cannot control other people or external events, no matter how much you want to. It's the paradox of control. The thing is, you won't be truly happy unless you're able to let go of what you can't control, learning to accept everything that happens to you and focusing on controlling what you can control, i.e. your perspectives and decisions.

The Art of Surrender

Why do we try to control everything in our lives? Well, you probably don't consciously mean to. The problem is that human beings are anxious and fearful, which is what we've discussed throughout this book. To realize that we're simply small beings on a massive planet flying through space with experiences and situations constantly being thrown at us from all directions is frankly terrifying and can cause an existential crisis. How are you supposed to find meaning and purpose in such chaos?

If you don't have control over things, then it's all going to spiral, and you won't know what will happen. For example, you choose to have control by not going on a date with someone you like because you're scared of being rejected. You prevent yourself from taking the risk of going on a date because you can stay in control and not get hurt by the unknown. Now think about all the other areas of your life where you hold yourself back, get angry and upset when things don't go your way, or are in the hands of other people, such as someone getting the promotion you were working towards.

It's so easy to feel bitter and stressed over such decisions, but it's entirely within your power to brush it off by accepting that the promotion wasn't meant to be and focusing your attention on bettering yourself in other areas. It's through making perspective changes like this that you'll be able to find peace and happiness throughout your life.

How exactly do you surrender? Let's cover some tips you need to know.

Don't Blame Others

It's so easy to get frustrated with things going on in your life and then blaming others, but as we've discussed, people are always going to do what they're going to do, and you only have control over your perspective and reactions . In other words, you need to stop blaming others and instead focus on yourself and what you can control.

Victimizing yourself because of the bad things that happen to you doesn't solve anything, but perpetuates the negative, overthinking patterns you have because it makes you feel out of control. You feel useless and incapable, waiting for someone else to come into your life to solve your problems, which is never a good long-term solution.

Basically, it's up to you to be responsible for the happiness and peace in your life. Once you accept responsibility and start doing things for yourself, you can start living the life you want, in full control of the things you can control. The actions of others have nothing to do with it. Dealing with people is just another essential, unavoidable part of life.

Decide to Let Go

This is easier said than done, but making the conscious decision to let go of something can do so much for your state of mind and your perception. It's inspiring to stand up and say you're going to do something, but it's pure power to do it. Whether that's starting a new habit, letting go of an old one, embracing a new way of life, or letting someone close to you go, this is about letting go of the old and moving into something new.

If you want to make any change in your life, you will go through this transition period of letting something go and stepping into something new, and if you want it to work, you need to take it seriously. For example, if you're quitting smoking, you're letting go of your bad habits and embracing a new one.

When you decide on what you want to change, write it down, for example, *I am no longer a smoker. I have decided to let go of smoking. I understand that smoking is bad for my health, and*

I will be happier, healthier, and better off without it. By writing this decision, you are more likely to follow through with your actions because you're making your decision real and tangible.

Put the note somewhere you're going to see it every single day and dive in and motivate yourself with the message that you're going to let go of the past and move into the new and better future. This is what it truly means to grow as an individual.

Believe in the Process

You've probably heard of a phrase like this or something like *trust the journey*. There's no doubt that this concept is true. It's very normal for an individual to fear what's to come. It's that inner sense that tells us we're not in control of what will happen, and because of this uncertainty, we get scared. After all, what if it's bad? This is why so many people get stuck in a rut or stop themselves from pursuing their dreams. The potential risk of failure is too immobilizing.

Instead, take a moment to think about the bad things that have happened in your life, especially those that have been outside of your control, and realize that you're here, having made it to the other side and everything is okay. You did that. You made it. Even if you're going through tough times now, you made it before, you'll make it again, and these bad times won't last forever.

Going through hard times helps you to appreciate and be grateful for the things you have and the parts of life that make you happy. I knew a friend who was diagnosed with cancer, and while terminal, he told me a month or so before he passed that although it was a terrible experience and he wouldn't wish it on anybody, it was amazing in a surreal way because it showed him what really mattered in life. He told me how careers, cars, big televisions, and fancy vacations didn't matter to him. With his wife, friends, and family around him, he discovered that the connections he had with these people were the most beautiful things.

Trust in your journey because it's going to teach you everything you need to know. As much as it may feel like it, you're not alone in your experiences, and you can bet that at least one other person has gone through something similar. They survived. You will too, and more often than not, you're going to be better off.

On that note, let's move away from acknowledging that there are things in life you can't control and delve into the areas of finding peace in your day-to-day life. Finding your peace is a process, especially since you have conditioned thoughts and feelings about the world and people. Instead of feeling pressured, judging the world, or trying to control everything, this next chapter is all about finding peace, the space in which you'll find happiness and satisfaction in the world.

METHOD 23

...& Finding Peace With Everything Else

Finding true balance—wouldn't that be the dream? With so much stress, anxiety, and other related issues prevalent in modern life, you're probably wondering whether it's possible to find peace. Perhaps you reserved the idea of real peace to something only someone like an enlightened buddha could obtain. While some elements of that may or may not be true, there are certainly ways you can introduce peace in your life, and this is connected with everything we spoke about in the last chapter about finding peace with what you can and can't control.

We've already covered so many things you could implement to find peace in your life, especially when it comes to calming your overthinking mind, but to tie things off nicely before we set off onto some more actionable points, we're going to briefly go through some of the most impactful ways you can find peace in your day-to-day life.

Set Boundaries and Limits

If you don't have boundaries and limits with yourself in all areas of your life, you're always going to be torn between options, and your life will be chaotic. This could be limiting yourself with how much food you're eating or how much money you're spending (aka, managing your budget). It may be setting limits on how much time you're spending with certain people or how much time you're spending on social media.

If you don't have time to do something, then set the boundary of saying no. If you need some time to yourself for whatever reason, they know that this is a priority you should be taking. Without setting boundaries and limits to guide you, you'll be stressed, and life will feel chaotic.

Slow Down Your Life

We live in a fast-paced world. You post a photo, and you get likes. You order a new product, and it's delivered the next day. You text someone, and they text back instantly. Everything is happening, and it's happening now, and it's no wonder that we feel stressed. However, even with your boss breathing down your neck about your impending deadline, you can find absolute peace of mind and peace of being by slowing everything down.

This stressful, fast-paced daily life forces you to speed up and get things done quicker, allowing you to move onto the next thing. But this is where you should slow down. I mean this literally. Slow down and do certain tasks in your life slower and with purpose. Instead of rushing to get everything done as fast as possible, take a moment to stop and enjoy what you're doing, and this can apply to mundane tasks such as folding laundry or driving.

This is one of those instant-result recommendations. Start by slowing down your breathing. Instead of rushing through these words, take a moment to really appreciate language and the fact you can read this and understand it. Look out your window or around the room and focus on all the details that you perhaps never notice.

Notice colors and areas of shadow. Notice the air and the sounds around. Take a moment to take it all in. Instead of jumping out or reaching for your phone and scrolling every now and then, reach for it gently, and when you're scrolling, stop to look at posts and take in what they are about. It may seem or feel silly at first, but it's so much more peaceful, and it's a great way to really appreciate your life and everything in it. It's the literal definition of *stopping to smell the flowers*. Stop to take in the details of the world, no matter how small or what kind of journey you're on.

Have Some Escape Time

If you're always on the go and you never take a breather, nor to have time to yourself, you're going to feel chaotic, crazy, and stressed. What you need is some time off to *do you*, doing things you enjoy. Whether you're reading a book, playing an instrument, watching your favorite show, going for a walk, or going out in your garden, take time to relax and unwind from the stresses you face in your daily life.

You can't be on the go in your life the entire time. You need to unwind and take a break to recharge your batteries and look after your mental health. You can't rev a car in the red the entire time because you'll destroy the engine. The most fuel-efficient way to look after your car and prolong its lifespan is by going slow and steady, and this means having breaks.

Ideally, you find *you* time. You might enjoy social media or calling up a friend, and, do this from time to time. However, you must learn to get comfortable being alone and spending time with yourself. It will help you refocus and reapply yourself to be more productive and connected with other aspects in your life.

Take Things One Step at a Time

Some people take pride in their ability to multitask, and while there's a time and place for multitasking, it's not the best way of doing things. Think about times in your life when you're busy and have a million things on your to-do list. You have calls to make, emails to answer, kids to take to school, deadlines to meet, food to buy, meals to cook, classes to attend, and more.

When you're trying to do all these things, your mind feels fried and overwhelmed. It's where stress comes from. To prevent this from happening and to find peace, you need to slow things down and take everything one step at a time. I'm not saying you shouldn't think about something when you're doing something else, but be balanced with it.

When you're shopping for food, focus on what you're doing and the environment you're in. A fantastic piece of advice is always to remember that there is going to be a tomorrow. Of course, you need to prioritize your life. You can't pick your kids up from school tomorrow when it needs to be done today, but get used to time management and spacing out what's important. There's no point in worrying about the exam you're taking next week if you're not going to do anything about it now. This is what it means to take control of what you can control.

This is a rule I like to live my life by. If you can't or won't do anything about it now, then it's not worth thinking about. Say I have some writing to do. I'm not going to worry about it until I the time I sit down and write. That's not saying I won't have ideas in the meantime, and of course, I'll write them down if they come to me, but for the bulk of the task, I will dedicate my time and energy to the right time.

For now, this should be enough food for thought when it comes to finding peace in your life, and combining everything you've learned in the previous chapter, you should be able to let go of everything that you can't control and grasp what you can. It's a matter of perspective, and even reading this chapter should be enough to get you thinking in your day-to-day life. You've perhaps already had it so far where a lesson from this book has popped into your head and helped you view life in a different, and hopefully more positive and grounded way.

There's an incredibly powerful way you can change your thinking to bring real joy, peace, happiness, and satisfaction in your life, and this is by taking a moment to think about your life in a new way.

Method 24

Discovering the Joys of Gratitude

Speak to anyone who's changed their life in some way, and you'll hear the same story. While the details may differ, at some point, they'll express gratitude for something or someone in their life that helped them get this far. This is what everybody does when they accept awards and say thank you to the people in their life that helped them get there. This is an act of acknowledging others and showing gratitude.

You've probably heard of gratitude, and no, it's not just the tip you give to your waiter. Gratitude is a practice that you can implement into your daily life, actively making sure you're paying attention to who and what's around you, and you're being grateful for its or their in your life. As Ferris Bullier states in the hit teen movie, *Ferris Bueller's Day Off*:

"Life moves pretty fast. If you don't stop and look around once in a while, you could miss it."

This is not an attack, but many of us go through life without appreciating what we have. In many respects, it's not even our fault, as we live in a world where we're conditioned to always chase something. We're told that we're never going to be happy until we have the new phone, the new car, that special vacation or those fashionable clothes. We're told we need to do this or buy this, and we end up craving everything that we don't have instead of being grateful and happy with what we do have.

This is the very basis of practicing gratitude. It's about taking a moment to be happy with what you have rather than craving more. Sure, it's easy to get caught up with comparing yourself to other people. You may compare yourself to celebrities in one moment and wish you had access to all the amazing things they have, but you could then compare yourself to people living in third-world countries in poverty to realize that you don't have it so bad.

While this sort of thinking can be eye-opening, it's far more beneficial to not compare yourself to other people but instead focus on yourself and how you feel about yourself. In my own life, focusing on myself and taking time to be grateful for what I had and what experiences I was going through, rather than constantly comparing myself to others and what they had, had my happiness slowly increasing. I was happy for the little things and mindfully noticed that my cravings for new things started to fade away.

It took a while, and even now, I know my habits aren't perfect. I constantly find myself on Instagram or Facebook, and I'll see a new phone or just some random gadget that doesn't do a lot, but I find myself wanting it. I'll look at my old phone and think, *man, I wish I had that new one with a better camera so I could take nice pictures.* Fortunately, thanks to my habits and practices, I can catch myself in the act and remind myself that these aren't things I truly need. Sure, if I need a new phone and want a nice one for the features it offers, that doesn't mean I'll deny myself. It just means I'm making that decision with thought and mindfulness, rather than feeling jealous or needy and getting it because of that.

Regardless, through trial and error, reading a lot of research, and listening to many expert opinions over the years, I managed to develop my own practices and mindsets that have helped me stay grateful. Before we jump into the practices, here's a very quick rundown of the scientific benefits gratitude can bring into your life.

The Benefits of a Gratitude Mindset

The benefits of gratitude have been studied and researched endlessly over the last few decades, and the results have always come out the same and claim the same or at least a similar message. Gratitude is very good for you and can do wonders for both your mental and physical health.

For example, a 2004 and a 2017 study found that gratitude not only boosts your overall sense of wellbeing and happiness, but it can do wonders for the capabilities of your immune system and can actively help you fight off illnesses and diseases. The 2017 study specifically proved that gratitude could actively reduce your risk of heart failure.

Gratitude practices can improve your mental health. A 2003 study found that gratitude can help improve your overall mood, while a 2020 study found that regular gratitude practices helped reduce symptoms of anxiety and depression. These benefits impact every aspect of your life, most notably your relationships. One study showed that a partner can demonstrate gratitude for something their partner has said or done and that this improved overall relationship satisfaction levels and overall happiness in less than 24 hours.

Of course, all of these have one main benefit in common, which is the core of this part of the book. Being grateful and practicing gratitude makes you happy. Even if you're not the most optimistic person in the world, practicing gratitude has been proven to help cultivate an optimistic perspective, allowing you to reap the benefits that come with this kind of mindset.

How to Bring Gratitude into Your Life

How can you practice grateful in your own life? It's easy to think about everything with gratitude. As you're reading this, you could easily think, *oh yes, I'm grateful for my house and my car and my family. I'm grateful I have a job and have food in the cupboards and so on,* but when you see someone buying a new car, and it makes you want one, and you actively feel sad that you don't have it, it's then that you really want your gratitude practices to kick in.

Much like everything else we've spoken about in this book, you'll experience these benefits when you start to make gratitude a regular, habitual part of your life. This means practicing it each and every day to the point where you don't even need to think about being grateful during the times you need to, it just happens naturally. It's the actions that can get you to the next point.

Be Grateful for Everything

It's easy to fall into the habit of only being grateful for the big things in life. This could be the presence of a person, a week's vacation, a roof over your head, a lottery win, or a celebration like a wedding or a birthday. Practicing gratitude during these times is easy because everyone is feeling it.

However, to reap the benefits, you'll want to start being grateful for everything you can be grateful for. This means paying attention to the things happening in your life and your minute-to-minute experiences and being grateful for them. This could be something simple like enjoying the sun coming out for the day or even the stillness that a rainy day can bring.

Maybe you received a text or a letter from someone you care about, or you just had a nice day in general. Maybe the day was average, but nothing bad happened, so you can be grateful for this. It really doesn't matter what happens or what you're going through; get into the habit of reminding yourself to be grateful. Even on my way to get my morning coffee this morning, I came across a dog who leaped up at me and gave me the biggest, friendliest lick. I was so grateful for such a happy experience and spent the rest of the day with a smile on my face.

Be Grateful for the Hard Times

As we've already discussed, it's easy to be grateful during the good times but easy to forget during the hard times. If you want to be truly grateful and happy in your life, learn how to be grateful for the difficulties, obstacles, and challenges you come across during your daily life. Challenges are important because they teach you great lessons and give you opportunities to become and grow into the best version of yourself.

Without these challenges, you would be stagnant, and you would always be the same person. You would never grow, and when a difficulty came along, you're going to struggle so much because you won't know how to deal with it since you wouldn't have learned the lesson.

Even if you're not going through anything now, take a moment to think about all the hard times and difficulties you've been through in your life, and how many lessons you've learned along the way, and how these experiences have shaped you into the person you are today. You may be holding onto some bitterness or resentment to the things you've been through, but learning to be grateful for them will help you let go and move on from them.

Keep a Gratitude Journal

Yes, we're back with another entry that asks you to keep a journal or diary about your life. However, you should already know that writing about your life helps you understand how important it is to you. Writing your thoughts turns your thoughts from being just thoughts into a real medium and a tangible object, and the same benefits apply to gratitude.

Take some time out of your day to write down all the things you are grateful for throughout your day. You could do this at the end of the day or when the things you're grateful for happen. It doesn't matter; all that matters is that you do it. The act of writing not only helps cement your gratitude, but also helps you develop your abilities to spot more things to be grateful for.

Because you're on the lookout for things to write down, you'll be far more observant of the little things that happen that make you happy that you would have otherwise missed.

Share Your Gratitude With Others

One of my favorite quotes from the popular movie *Into the Wild* is by the main character Chris, who leaves his comfortable, modern life to live off the land in the wilderness. However, his dying words, scribbled in his diary after eating poisonous berries were: "Happiness is only real when shared." This quote has stuck with me since the first time I watched the based-on-real-life movie.

When it comes to happiness, you'll get the most out of your emotions when you're sharing them with other people. This is why when you go to a concert to see a band, and the atmosphere is nothing short of euphoric, the whole experience feels amazing. It's times like this when people have some of the best and most memorable moments of their lives.

It's because you're in a situation where you're sharing the same experiences with people, even though they're strangers, and you're all grateful to be in such a great environment, that the overall atmosphere becomes electric. You can use this same logic in your day-to-day life.

Share your experiences and gratitude with others, and you'll see that it's contagious. For example, imagine you're camping with friends, and you wake up early to see the most beautiful sunrise. When you exclaim how beautiful and how amazing the sunrise seems, and everyone else agrees, you're sharing your gratitude for the moment, and everyone else feels it too. This cocktail of connectedness and gratitude can be the source of so much happiness.

You don't have to wait for moments like that. Even if you're at work and you have a good week, sharing your gratitude for being a part of such a great team, or something simple like sharing lunch with someone on your break can be a source of happiness.

To summarize, observe the going-ons in your life. This may feel like a lot right now, but if you've been following through and implementing the things you've learned in this book, your mind should feel quieter. Since you're overthinking less and no longer consumed with thoughts and feelings, you can use the space created in your thoughts to focus on gratitude and happiness.

Just remember, learning and implementing all these tips and strategies can take time, so learn to be patient with yourself and watch the benefits grow.

Method 25

The Simple Act of Setting Up Your Day

This is perhaps an interesting chapter title, but it is an essential practice that literally changed my life. I spent my days waking up and then struggling to find my footing, what I was doing, and what the day was going to be about. As we've discussed already, this unorganized and chaotic way of living life was causing me a great deal of stress and anxiety that led to more overthinking.

Then I learned about morning routines. How you spend and follow through with your morning is so important because it quite literally sets you up for the rest of your day. If you have a bad start to your morning, aka waking up on the wrong side of the bed, then the rest of your day can also be ruined, or at least it can take a tremendous amount of energy to turn things around.

On the other hand, if you take time to set up your mornings and have them serve you, then you can set yourself up for a productive, satisfying, and peaceful day. Years ago, I would wake up about twenty minutes before leaving for work. I wouldn't have breakfast and would spend most of the day hungry. I would be tired and stressed and distracted, and the days would be a blur, leaving me feeling exhausted and out of touch with myself.

However, changing my morning routine, creating healthy habits, and setting them in stone gave me productivity and purpose. It allowed me to have structure and meaning. It always took the thinking out of my mornings. I knew exactly what I was doing and when I had to do it, meaning there was no stress. I just had to go through the motions, which allowed me to focus my energy on facing the challenges of the day, whether that was work-based, creative work, or whatever it was I had to do.

Of course, the benefits of having a morning routine are well-researched and are thoroughly documented. There are studies that prove morning routines provide the following benefits:

- Increased productivity
- Lower stress levels
- Improved memory capabilities
- Better, more connected relationships
- Higher energy levels
- The ability to create healthier habits
- Improved mood and overall feelings of happiness
- More feeling of control over your life

Let's explore some of the best ways to introduce a morning routine into your life.

How to Set Yourself Up for a Great Day

Let's go through the process. This is the process I developed, tweaked, and changed over the years, but it's what works for me. You could follow my approach to a tee, or you can tweak it to make your own. Remember, it's all about figuring out what works for you.

I get up nice and early, usually setting my alarm for 6 am. Some people will start at 7, and some as early as five. This is determined by your personal preference. Six is an excellent middle ground for me. Early starts are great because they are an opportunity to have more time to get everything done. If you get up late and you're rushing around because you have to leave for work and don't have enough time, everything is stressful. Get up early, and you can take things at a much more leisurely and calm pace, allowing yourself to warm up into the day and find your footing.

Make Your Bed

Making your bed as one of the first things you do when you wake up changes everything, and for many reasons. It's a simple act, but before you've even left your bedroom, you've already achieved a task. Now, in your mind, you've already set yourself up for a beautiful day where your bedroom is looking lovely and tidy; therefore your mind is tidy, and you've put yourself in a state of mind where you're getting stuff done.

Look, don't take it from me. Be your own proof. When you wake up tomorrow morning, make your bed. It takes less than two minutes, and you'll see how much of a positive effect it will have on your life.

Develop a Standard Routine

After making your bed, it's time to move onto the next aspects of your morning routine, and this can be whatever you want it to be. However, whatever actions you choose, you need to make sure you choose one that benefits you. I've tried implementing a yoga practice, reading, having a morning coffee outside while reading the news, meditating, journaling, and going for a run, among other activities.

What do you want to do? Do you want to learn a language? Maybe get up, pour coffee and start your Duolingo session. If you want to get healthy, go for a run or at least a walk before you do anything else. If you want to be more organized, start by writing a to-do list or tidy up your home and get everything in order.

It's always best to start with the things you must do, such as brushing your teeth, having a shower, and washing your face. Then add in the extras you want while making sure you have time to do everything. If you wake up at six and need to leave for work at half-past eight, fit your activities into those two and a half hours. Plan and get organized so you know what you're doing and when. The more thought you can take out of your morning, the more you'll get done and can stick to your new routines.

Drink a Glass of Water

Imagine going through an eight-hour day and not drinking a single drink, not even a glass of water. Well, if you're getting enough sleep every night, this is exactly what your body is going through every single night. Sure, you're resting, but your body still gets dehydrated, which is why it's essential to make getting yourself a drink one of the first things you do every morning as soon as you wake up.

This helps your body wake up, hydrates you, and provides other benefits like improving your digestive processes and helps your body to filter out toxins. Make your life easier by leaving a glass of water next to your bed, so it's easily accessible the moment you wake up, once again taking the thinking part out of your morning and instead of making it easy for you to benefit from positive habits.

Eat Something Healthy

Finally, you want to continue your healthy habits by making sure you're drinking and eating healthy. It's easy to opt for something easy in the morning when you don't have time to sort yourself out and are still tired, but when you're waking up early and have time, you have time to put more effort into what you're eating.

When I used to rush out to work, I'd grab something from a cafe, which was usually greasy and not ideal for my health or weight, especially when I was eating it every day. After adopting a morning routine, I was able to take control of my diet and improve my overall health.

To summarize, having a morning routine can change everything for you, and it's another way you can control what's going on in your life and be proactive in becoming a better you. All the studies and research that this is one of the best decisions you can make in your life to become the best version of yourself, so be your own proof and give it a go!

METHOD 26

Working on Habits That Will Take Care of You

Carrying on from the last chapter, although working on a morning routine will do wonders for your life and can drastically improve your overall peace and happiness, it's not the only area of your life where you can make improvements. Your habits and lifestyle choices affect every part of your life, and since your actions and decisions are the main things you can control, this is an area you're going to need to think about.

This is what this chapter is about. We're talking about the proven self-care, self-development, and habitual practices you can do to look after yourself. If you're looking after yourself and showing yourself some proper love and attention, you're going to be feeling your best as you head into any situation or experience. This is the way to become the best version of yourself!

I'm going to make this chapter as actionable as possible because you've heard some of it before, you may need a refresher on some, and some may be completely new, so figure out which ones you resonate with and enjoy how they make you feel!

Get Outside

As humans, we connect with nature in a surreal, instinctual way, but thanks to the modern world, it's easy to find ourselves more disconnected from it than ever before. Ever wondered why we put natural wallpapers as the backgrounds to our phones and computers? It's that inner craving we have to be in and around nature. In fact, science has proven many times that you'll be far happier if you spend at least a little time in nature as and when you can.

Science shows that being in nature can make you happier, more peaceful, and releases endorphins, and can even boost your creativity levels. Start simple and visit a green space. Even if you're going for a quick walk to your local park, this is enough to feel the benefits. You could even try working out outside or spend some time reading in the sun.

Whatever it is you do, and however you spend your time, the trick is to try to get into a daily practice of spending at least half an hour in nature where you can.

Enjoy Something Beautiful Everyday

Life is mundane unless you actively put the things you enjoy in front of you. Perhaps surprisingly, one of the biggest and most significant changes I made in my life was to spend time listening to a song I enjoyed every single day and doing nothing else. Whether I was standing in my bedroom, sitting on the sofa, or walking to work, I would listen to whatever song made me happy at the time and would instantly feel the smile appear on my face.

Whatever it is you enjoy, whether it's music or a YouTube creator, art, a magazine, photography, or something else that makes you smile, make sure you're taking time out every day to enjoy it. Sure, what you love can change from day to day or month to month, but it's that act of saying *I love this, so no matter what, I'm going to allow myself to enjoy it* that will make you happy. This is the process of literally giving yourself self-love and becoming happier and healthier because of it.

Indulge in your Releases

Sometimes, it's not going to matter how mindful you are, how in control of your decisions you've become, or how peaceful you've found yourself in your day-to-day life. Sometimes the world can just get the better of you, and you'll find yourself in a place where you need to let off some steam. This is perhaps the point you've been waiting for, because yes, sometimes you do need to indulge to get yourself back on track.

While there are healthier ways of dealing with things aside from binge eating, binge-watching, going for a night out on the town, or even something as simple as swearing, sometimes you just need to do it to get it out of your system to feel better. If you're at a point in your life where you need to let something go, or you need a day off, do it. You're a human being, not a machine.

Your habits and looking after yourself are important, but that doesn't mean you should make yourself miserable in the process. If you need to go out and eat a whole pizza by yourself, then do it. However, the trick here is to make sure you're doing it in such a way that you remain in control. This means picking yourself up and dusting yourself off and getting back on the habit horse as quickly as possible.

Forgive yourself for needing to do what you need to do, don't beat yourself up over it, and move on.

Connect with Someone

Human connection is everything, and enjoying those connections is bound to make you feel happy and complete. Connection is one of the best self-help tips you can follow. Fortunately, even if you're introverted or don't have many people in your life, the trick is to do what you can and do what works for you.

Bear in mind that physical contact is a big part of connection. Everything from a cuddle or hug to sexual intercourse has been proven repeatedly to provide many mental health and physical benefits that will do you a world of good. Of course, these aren't options in all situations, but it's certainly worth thinking about.

Go On a Trip

There's no doubt that travels are good for the soul, so if you haven't gone anywhere for a while, which is almost certainly the case for most people since the COVID-19 pandemic hit, then it could be time to see some different walls and explore some new places by taking a trip away. Getting away from your hometown at least once a year is highly recommended, especially if you're visiting a new culture because you'll be able to make memories with your family or friends, diversify your mind, subject yourself to some new perspectives, and have fun.

What's more, science thankfully backs up this notion. Studies show that going away for a trip can help improve and restore your overall levels of focus, boost creativity, reduce your risk of heart disease, and so much more. If you've been looking for an excuse to get away, this is it.

Life can be hard. It's hard for everyone at different stages, but that doesn't mean that life can't be enjoyed. You can't have good without the bad, light without the dark, and you wouldn't even know when life is good without having the harder times to compare them to. If everything was good, then life would just be average and bland.

These little habits that we've discussed come down to one core point: to be kind to yourself. The problem with stress, anxiety, and overthinking is that you learn to hate yourself. You hate that your mind won't shut up and won't let you be. You can get bitter and resentful that you're never happy while the rest of the world seems to be living it up, and this is why so many of us fall into unhealthy habits like not sleeping, smoking, drinking, taking drugs, and so on.

Take a step back and learn to be kind to yourself, or at least try doing things and get involved in activities that allow you to be kind to yourself. Like every other skill in life, it can take time and a bit of practice, but you'll start to see the results soon.

METHOD 27

Truly Live in the Moment

And here we are—the final chapter of this book. By now, you've learned pretty much everything you need to know when it comes to becoming the best version of yourself, or at least the version of yourself that will continue to grow no matter what. However, there's one important consideration you need to make - the age-old saying you've heard of but perhaps haven't realized the importance of it until now.

This is the act of living in the moment.

When you think of living in the moment, what comes to mind? Do you think about people who cliff dive or seek other adrenaline rushes or people that take the plunge because they believe we all only live once? Living in the moment seems to have this kind of mentality attached to it, but while this idea of living in the moment is close, it's the entire message.

When you're in a state of overthinking, stress, or anxiety, your head is not in the moment. You're either regretting or overthinking something that's happened or anticipating the future. Either way, your mind isn't right here. Think about when you're having a panic attack, and you use the 5,4,3,2,1 method. You're doing what you can to bring your mind back to the present moment.

This is what it means to truly live in the moment. It's to be utterly free of overthinking. Perhaps this is why people associate the phrase with living on the edge. It's because you're in the moment and you're not thinking about the consequences, nor worrying about the future or what people think. You're just there, thriving off pure instinct and happiness and going with the flow.

Fortunately, there's not really any new action you need to take or techniques you need to learn that haven't been discussed in this book. Whether it's meditating, changing your mindset and perspective, taking control of your decisions, or looking after yourself, every technique in this book will help to take you one step closer to being able to live in the moment.

However, if you want a takeaway from this chapter, and indeed what I believe to be a great way to finish off and close this book, it's this.

You are not your thoughts. You are the watcher of your thoughts. You are your consciousness. Your mind is but a tool, just like your hand and feet are tools. Your mind is simply a complex tool that aims to solve problems and keep you alive. You are not your past, nor are you your future.

You are you. The only you that has ever existed. You've never not been in the present moment. You were never living yesterday nor tomorrow, but always now. This might not make a lot of sense, and it may feel like an abstract concept right now, but allow yourself to process those words. Apply the lessons to your life. Next time you catch yourself overthinking, feeling scared or sad, unsure of what you're doing, or anxious about some big life event, remember, these are only thoughts.

They are not you. You are simply a being that experiences those thoughts.

Final Thoughts

Phew. That was a mammoth amount of information, but here we are at the end of the journey. Well, the end of this part of the journey, but with the information you've learned throughout the previous chapters, it's safe to say that really your journey is just beginning. One final time, just because it's so important to remember, I'll say that this kind of self-development journey takes time.

It takes time to figure out what works for you. It takes time to let go of the past and old ways of thinking. It takes time to embrace and become accustomed to the new and growing versions of yourself, and it takes time for your new habits to form and to let them settle in. Be kind to yourself and trust the process. Your journey, no matter where you go and what you do, will be full of ups and downs. That's just the natural flow of life.

Forgive yourself. You're going to make mistakes, and you're going to relapse from time to time. You'll make mistakes, and you'll learn from them. That's okay. There's no need to rush, and there's no need to panic. You are making progress every time you take a step. Sometimes it feels like you're going backward, but you're not. Everything is going to be okay.

Now go and be the best version of yourself, and remember, the world owes you nothing, and nobody will do anything for you. It's up to you to make the change, but fortunately, you already have everything you're ever going to need right here, right now. You just need to take that first step.

I hope you've enjoyed reading this book, and there are at least some aspects of it that you've learned something new from. I understand that some of the lessons are ones you've already heard before, but hopefully, some are new, and you can apply them to your own life, or at least let them act as reminders for what you need to do.

I massively enjoyed writing this book as it acted as a summary of the last few years of my life and all the lessons I've learned and has given me a chance to think about what other areas I needed to work on. Most importantly, it allows me to exercise myself as a writer and helps me to walk the path that gives me the most purpose. I would like to take this moment to say that if you feel like this book gave you anything, then I would love to hear from you. You can do this by leaving me a review from wherever got the copy from. Positive or negative, I want to hear what you've got to say so I can continue on my path to becoming the best writer and person I can be.

With that, I hope to hear from you soon and will see you in the next one. Enjoy your journey, and I can't wait for you to embrace who you were born to be. Now go take that first step.

Thank you

Before you go, I just wanted to say thank you for purchasing my book.

There are many books on the same topic, but you took a chance and chose this one.

So, thank you for choosing me and for reading this book all the way to the end.

Now, I wanted to ask you for a small favor. **Could you please consider posting a review for the book? Reviews are the easiest way to support an independent author like me.**

Your feedback will help me continue to create books that will help you achieve the results you want. So, if you enjoyed it, please let me know.

References

Time. 2021. *Here's How Happy Americans Are Right Now*. [online] Available at: <https://time.com/4871720/how-happy-are-americans/> [Accessed 11 August 2021].

Nami.org. 2021. *Mental Health By the Numbers | NAMI: National Alliance on Mental Illness*. [online] Available at: <https://nami.org/mhstats> [Accessed 11 August 2021].

KERA News. 2021. *How Overthinking Can Affect Mental And Physical Health*. [online] Available at: <https://www.keranews.org/health-science-tech/2019-07-12/how-overthinking-can-affect-mental-and-physical-health> [Accessed 11 August 2021].

Urmc.rochester.edu. 2021. *5-4-3-2-1 Coping Technique for Anxiety*. [online] Available at: <https://www.urmc.rochester.edu/behavioral-health-partners/bhp-blog/april-2018/5-4-3-2-1-coping-technique-for-anxiety.aspx> [Accessed 11 August 2021].

Jennie Marie Battistin, L. and Jennie Marie Battistin, L., 2021. *5,4,3,2,1 Method to Reduce Anxiety — Hope Therapy Center*. [online] Hope Therapy Center. Available at: <https://www.hope-therapy-center.com/single-post/2016/04/06/54321-method-to-reduce-anxiety> [Accessed 11 August 2021].

Digitalcommons.odu.edu. 2021. [online] Available at: <https://digitalcommons.odu.edu/cgi/viewcontent.cgi?article=1054&context=chs_pubs> [Accessed 11 August 2021].

Citeseerx.ist.psu.edu. 2021. *Download Limit Exceeded*. [online] Available at: <http://citeseerx.ist.psu.edu/viewdoc/download?doi=10.1.1.913.3731&rep=rep1&type=pdf> [Accessed 11 August 2021].

Uofmhealth.org. 2021. *Stress Management: Breathing Exercises for Relaxation | Michigan Medicine*. [online] Available at: <https://www.uofmhealth.org/health-library/uz2255> [Accessed 11 August 2021].

Adaa.org. 2021. *Facts & Statistics | Anxiety and Depression Association of America, ADAA*. [online] Available at: <https://adaa.org/understanding-anxiety/facts-statistics> [Accessed 11 August 2021].

Uofmhealth.org. 2021. *Stress Management: Doing Progressive Muscle Relaxation | Michigan Medicine*. [online] Available at: <https://www.uofmhealth.org/health-library/uz2225> [Accessed 11 August 2021].

WebMD. 2021. *Progressive Muscle Relaxation for Stress and Insomnia*. [online] Available at: <https://www.webmd.com/sleep-disorders/muscle-relaxation-for-stress-insomnia> [Accessed 11 August 2021].

Sleepfoundation.org. 2021. *Sleep Statistics - Facts and Data About Sleep 2020 | Sleep Foundation*. [online] Available at: <https://www.sleepfoundation.org/how-sleep-works/sleep-facts-statistics> [Accessed 11 August 2021].

Medbroadcast.com. 2021. *Lifestyle tips for managing anxiety - Mental Health - MedBroadcast.com*. [online] Available at: <https://www.medbroadcast.com/channel/mental-health/treating-anxiety/lifestyle-tips-for-managing-anxiety> [Accessed 11 August 2021].

Schulze, A., 2021. *5 Easy Steps to Changing Your Thinking Using Cognitive Behavioral Therapy (CBT)*. [online] Groffandassociates.com. Available at: <https://groffandassociates.com/2017/10/12/5-easy-steps-to-changing-your-thinking-using-cognitive-behavioral-therapy-cbt/> [Accessed 11 August 2021].

Hall, J., 2021. *10 Ways To Help Others That Will Lead You To Success*. [online] Forbes. Available at: <https://www.forbes.com/sites/johnhall/2013/05/26/10-ways-to-help-others-that-will-lead-you-to-success/?sh=1ca04942bce8> [Accessed 11 August 2021].

Healthline. 2021. *Positive Self-Talk: Benefits and Techniques*. [online] Available at: <https://www.healthline.com/health/positive-self-talk#examples-of-positive-self--talk> [Accessed 11 August 2021].

Let Go of Control: How to Learn the Art of Surrender. (2015, March 27). Tiny Buddha. https://tinybuddha.com/blog/let-go-of-control-how-to-learn-the-art-of-surrender/

Free Yourself By "Letting Go" of What You Can't Control. (2011, July 10). You Have a Calling. https://youhaveacalling.com/emotional-health/free-yourself-by-letting-go-of-what-you-cant-control

How to Learn to Let Go of What You Can't Control. (2019, October 8). Lifehack. https://www.lifehack.org/847748/learn-to-let-go

Redwine, L. S., Henry, B. L., Pung, M. A., Wilson, K., Chinh, K., Knight, B., Jain, S., Rutledge, T., Greenberg, B., Maisel, A., & Mills, P. J. (2016). Pilot Randomized Study of a Gratitude Journaling Intervention on Heart Rate Variability and Inflammatory Biomarkers in Patients With Stage B Heart Failure. *Psychosomatic Medicine*, 78(6), 667–676. https://doi.org/10.1097/psy.0000000000000316

Cregg, D. R., & Cheavens, J. S. (2020). Gratitude Interventions: Effective Self-help? A Meta-analysis of the Impact on Symptoms of Depression and Anxiety. *Journal of Happiness Studies.* https://doi.org/10.1007/s10902-020-00236-6

Cregg, D. R., & Cheavens, J. S. (2020). Gratitude Interventions: Effective Self-help? A Meta-analysis of the Impact on Symptoms of Depression and Anxiety. *Journal of Happiness Studies.* https://doi.org/10.1007/s10902-020-00236-6

APA PsycNet. (n.d.). Psycnet.apa.org. Retrieved August 11, 2021, from https://psycnet.apa.org/record/2010-10257-015

Salces-Cubero, I. M., Ramírez-Fernández, E., & Ortega-Martínez, A. R. (2018). Strengths in older adults: differential effect of savoring, gratitude and optimism on well-being. *Aging & Mental Health*, *23*(8), 1017–1024. https://doi.org/10.1080/13607863.2018.1471585

Marelisa. (2015, January 22). *Nine Morning Habits to Start the Day Right.* Daringtolivefully.com. https://daringtolivefully.com/morning-habits

Suttie, J. (2016, March 2). *How Nature Can Make You Kinder, Happier, and More Creative.* Greater Good. https://greatergood.berkeley.edu/article/item/how_nature_makes_you_kinder_happier_more_creative

Printed in Great Britain
by Amazon